26 WORDS

THAT CAN CHANGE YOUR LIFE

...A PRIMER TO HELP YOU HELP YOURSELF

PHILLIP BROWN

This book contains opinions and ideas of the author who is not a medical professional. Nor is he intending to dispense medical advice of any sort. Any such required assistance should be in consultation with a medical professional. The content of this book is general in nature and not specific to the reader's circumstances. The intent of the author is to share his experiences and ideas as to how they had an impact on him. In the event that you use any information in this book for your own purposes the author and the publisher assume no responsibility for your outcomes.

ISBN 978-0-9939006-0-0

Library of Congress Control Number Pending

Proudly printed in Canada

Online copies printed in the USA

Cover photography and graphics: Mike Wing www.wingstudios.ca

Cover design: Sarah Fairbairn www.sarahfairbairn.ca

With much appreciation to my awesome editor Susan Chilton www.susanchilton.com

To Emily - May you always be kind and receive kindness in return.

Take the road less traveled, as that can make all the difference.

To all those people who have been part of my life journey thus far, thank you.

To those who supported this new book, I express heartfelt appreciation.

26 WORDS

"The writing of *26 Words That Can Change Your Life* has changed mine. As I write, I learn about and challenge myself to be better."

Phillip Brown

A portion of the proceeds from the sale of this book will be donated to charitable causes. If you would like to have your charity participate, please email the author. phillipbrown@gracemedia.com

The author welcomes your questions or comments about *26 Words* by email at info@26words.com

TABLE OF CONTENTS

ABOUT THE AUTHOR

Phillip Brown lives and works in Kingston, Ontario, Canada. He loves life's challenges and joys and seeks to get as much as he can out of each minute of every day.

While writing *26 Words*, Phillip became a father for the first time. He realizes that he now really has to live up to what he writes about in this book.

He has a passion for being on or in the water and his free time is filled with adventure, sports and the performing arts.

Oh, and changing diapers.

Phillip is also the author of the novel *Critical Care*, a fictional medical thriller: www.criticalcare.ca.

Phillip welcomes your requests for speaking engagements, to get your audience fired up. He adds this comment:

"One of the great joys I have experienced in putting together the material for *26 Words* That Can Change Your Life has been the audience response to the words during my public speaking engagements. It was that feedback which made me feel I was onto something that people truly appreciated. I love doing a morning talk to get people engaged and ready for their day with new energy and new ideas as to how they will tackle what's ahead of them."

If you would like to have Phillip speak with your group, please connect with him at phillipbrown@gracemedia.com.

PREFACE

Star Trek was one of my all-time favorite television shows. In it, Captain James T. Kirk was always asking Dr. "Bones" McCoy to stretch his capabilities and help Kirk out of complex situations.

Such exchanges coined pop-culture phrases like, "Damn it, Jim, I'm a doctor, not a mechanic," or "Jim, I'm a doctor, not an engineer," or, "Jim, I'm a doctor, not a veterinarian."

In writing *26 Words That Can Change Your Life*, I feel compelled to say, "Damn it, friends, I'm a life observer, not a psychiatrist."

Most of what I have written is based on my experiences and I use metaphors liberally to try and share my message with you. While the stories here are mostly factual, I am not immune to adding the pepper of fiction to spice things up.

I must admit that I have always identified with good, old Captain Kirk. He never was one to walk away from a challenge or an opportunity to stretch, change, and grow to achieve a goal.

"Bones" McCoy, on the other hand, personifies that tendency within us to balk at change and resist the possibility that a challenge might actually be good for us.

In the opening of any Star Trek episode or movie, the voice-over talks about boldly going where no man has gone before.

I hope that I can stimulate you to go to places that you have yet to go, and to engage new beginnings and new frontiers within yourself.

INTRODUCTION

When I look back on my life, I can clearly see the path that I have taken, and I know that I am blessed to be here.

I easily could have perished as I sought thrills from external stimulation while avoiding any internal "infrastructure" growth.

By the mid 1990s, I'd had enough of the "me" that the world knew. I became serious about getting into and exposing the "me" that I knew and that had been shared with few people. I put my life at home and business on hold. Single and childless, I headed to Africa for a seven-month journey that changed my life.

Would I come back changed? Would I come back at all?

No one knew. Few cared.

The door of the Air Canada flight closed. The engines roared. My journey began.

I had no idea just how plugged up my heart, mind and soul were with the accumulated garbage of life thus far. I didn't realize the soul-cleansing power of time alone for reflection, on an ancient continent, devoid of most modern temptations.

Epiphanies can happen anywhere when we decide we are ready or need to let go of all we know and allow renewal to happen. My personal epiphany happened five months into my journey, while I was watching the sunrise from the top of Mount Kilimanjaro.

By then, I had finally stopped cramming stuff into my brain. Every day in Africa was so simple: get up at dawn, eat, read, relax, exercise, maybe have a small or larger adventure, be in bed by sunset. No booze. No fat. Little sugar. Usually no power for lights or any other modern convenience.

And — no internet!

I was truly unplugged from home, family and friends.

What happened during my months away was amazing, as the contents of my mind and soul began what I can only call a renewal process. Lifelong memories flooded forward. My poetry and story writing emerged again. Thoughts of people who had helped me along the way shone brightly in my mind as beacons on the path I had traced thus far.

What stood out most in my recollections was most often a simple gesture of kindness, a sentence, or — in some cases — just a sensitive, single word that had served as a guidepost or guardrail in my life.

Simple, yet powerful. Life-giving, in my case.

From a young age, I had struggled to get a positive response from the world around me, although my tools were blunt. When the response didn't match my wants, I would lash out, reinforcing to some that I was indeed getting what I deserved.

After Africa, I remember being on the T, the public transit in Boston. I was in travel mode — that place that brings out the best of us with strangers, and vice-versa. I chatted amiably with an older man for about 30 minutes. I can't actually recall what we discussed, but when we parted, he shook my hand warmly and said, "I have heard that in life we meet people for a reason, a season or a lifetime. I am not sure why I met you, Phillip, but I sure am glad I did."

For me, that summed it all up. That's what I had been searching for and that's what I mostly get from the world around me now. The journey back to "me" was rough, lonely, scary, and sometimes I just wanted to give up.

In *26 Words*, I hope to share with you some thoughts and lessons that I have worked hard to learn. I have paid my dues, so to speak, and perhaps I can save you some time or show you a shortcut to where you want to go.

What I have come to realize is that the smallest things can often have the greatest impact. For that reason, I have tried to keep it simple for you: no extra reading, no charts or graphs, nothing too complicated.

Just a few words and some ideas, in random order. Just pick a word, and start reading.

Pick a word for renewal or invigoration and work with it for a day, a week, or a year. Let it resonate.

Before we get going, I want to add that there are many life-changing words that arise from terrible situations that we humans endure. Just open the newspapers and there they are. By the time our life's journey is over, we will all deal with one or more losses or tragedies. I deliberately avoided the big, obvious, scary words that sometimes confront us. I am not presumptuous enough to think that my words trump others or are any more important than words that might already hold meaning for you. My simple hope is that in reading this book, one or more of my assortment may help you deal with, or heal from, a time when the hill you are climbing gets a bit steep and you could use a lift.

With that said, let's turn a page and get started.

ONE

YOU — are my first and last word.

Or should I say you "is" my first and last word?

You decide. From beginning to end, from morning to night, from birth to death, you are what counts above all else. This book is for and about you.

As you read, I suspect you will be thinking about all the people that you could now offer advice to or help fix. We are all great at seeing the flaws in others while staying blind to our own. Remember the adage that we dislike in others that which we dislike in ourselves? In other words, when you find yourself being critical of someone, stop and ask yourself: Are you criticizing something you find is weak or lacking in yourself?

I have a dear, long-term friend who is so full of foibles (as are we all) that I just love to tamper and tinker with him, imparting my wisdom, experience and ideas about how he can be better.

Does he really have that many foibles, or is it the emotional kaleidoscope through which I see my own that makes him seem wanting?

Sound familiar? Do you perhaps have such a friend or relative? Is it them or yourself that you are trying to fix?

Generally, my friend doesn't mind my meddling. However, a few years back, I pushed him to his breaking point and he burst out, "Stop trying to fucking fix me! I'm not broken!"

I replied, "I know, I know, but if you would just…"

His stare said it all. I shut my yap.

These days, I try to be more subtle.

Shortly after earning my private pilot's license, I was at a cocktail party and bumped into a family friend. He is a highly accomplished businessman, and intrepid traveler and explorer who has sailed the globe numerous times. He also became a helicopter pilot and flew well into his sixties.

"So, I hear you're a pilot," he said.

"Yes, as of just three months ago."

"What are you flying?"

"A Cessna 172 from the flying club."

He looked at me, through years of experience, and put his hand on my forearm. "Remember, there is no one more important than you. If you remember that, you will likely never die flying."

Interesting that he said "likely." I suppose that should have concerned me.

I regarded him for a few seconds, soaking in this little pearl. As a more seasoned pilot today, I now know much better what he meant that night. If I focus on my safety first and put aside all other agendas, pressure and temptations that come with flying, I will fly safely.

"Thank you," I said. "I appreciate you taking the time to share that thought and I promise to remember it."

Though we parted for other conversations, as I write this for you, that moment is etched in my mind. It is moments like that and simple words like that which inspired this book. A simple, elegant few seconds in time between two people, who might not otherwise have crossed paths, had a major impact on my flying and my life.

These moments happen, and will continue to happen to you, too. Who knows where they come from, but they are for you and your well-being and sustainability.

Are you listening?

Are you ready?

Will you see the magic and power in a word, gesture or sentence from a stranger you come across on a bus or plane, or maybe standing behind you in the grocery-store line?

You are the captain of your vessel. What do you imagine when I write that? A boat, train, plane, job, role, community volunteer, brother, sister, parent, friend or colleague?

Your vessel is you!

You are the President and CEO of YOU Inc.

What's your mission, vision and value statement?

How will you measure success for YOU Inc.?

What are your dreams, goals, challenges and aspirations?

Do you believe me when I tell you that you can accomplish whatever change you wish to in your life and achieve more than you ever thought possible? You can break bad habits, mend broken relationships, be the best friend, partner, employee, parent or leader that you wish to be. You can lose that weight, improve your health, and learn to sing or dance or play an instrument.

You can leave that bad relationship and start again. You can say no to abuse and move on. You can say yes to being the best you possible. You can express yourself artistically or write a book or travel to a distant land. You can change bad moods to good, make good moods better, and radiate that into your surroundings.

It starts every time you wake up, with a pledge to yourself as to how your day will go and what you will get out of it. It starts with saying "thank you" as your two feet hit the ground.

It continues with how you respond to each person and situation throughout your day. It is nourished by what you feed your body, mind and soul all day and evening long. It persists while you sleep, if you take a few moments, before you close your eyes, to appreciate you for what you accomplished that day.

Celebrate even the smallest successes and avoid beating yourself up for shortcomings.

Take baby steps.

Your character is likely to be defined by the accumulation of thousands of small deeds and positive steps of progress; few of us are defined through a momentary act of heroism. I suggest that waiting to one day become a hero will lead you to a false existence. It seems to me that heroes emerge when they are ready for their heroic moment, and those moments rarely present themselves.

Life isn't about balance, either; if 51 percent of the time you are good and 49 percent bad, it doesn't mean you pass. It doesn't work that way. The fact is that the better we get, the harder it is to continue to get better. Fortunately, the better we get, the more drive we seem to be given to achieve even more.

Think about the top athletes in the world. They spend untold hours trying to achieve the tiniest of improvements, like shaving a single stroke off a golf score or a few one-hundredths of a second off a swim, ski or track race. When you are at the beginning of improving anything, the first steps and early progress are easy. Sustaining growth, change and improvement is the hard part.

I am telling you this so you can be prepared for the joy of success, as well as the challenges, that come with this journey.

Quitting smoking for a week is easy. Losing five pounds is easy. Not drinking or getting high for a week is doable. Being nice to friends and family for a time seems simple. I am sure you get my drift.

What I am asking you to do, as I have done and continue to work on each day, is make sustained change, growth and improvement in your life and accept the setbacks and challenges that come with your efforts.

Why?

Because the rewards are mighty.

I once heard life described as mountains of sorrow and moments of glory, although I think that can apply to just about any project or journey.

You will have to find the joy in the work. No pain, no gain, so to speak.

I also want to remind you that there are three distinct phases in a change process.

The first phase is the excitement of beginning: "I am so excited about this decision to change and I have already seen progress!"

The second phase is, by far, the longest and hardest. That's when it seems that the world — in fact, the whole universe — is conspiring to stop you or hold you back: "I can't believe how hard this is! Why the heck am I doing this? This isn't worth it. I wish I'd never read that damn book!"

But wait; here comes the third phase: "I am so thankful, happy, proud and just darned pleased that I did that. I am not going back to where I was before."

Congratulations! You did it. Now move on to something else! Why stop now; you are just getting started.

An older woman went to her doctor for an annual check-up and chat.

"You're doing great," the doctor said. "You have had quite a life, haven't you? Do you have any regrets?"

"Yes," she replied without hesitation. "I always wished I had learned how to play the piano."

"Why don't you take lessons?"

"Do you know how old I will be by the time I learn how to play the piano?"

Her doctor smiled. "The same age you will be if you don't learn."

Famous actor and comedian, George Burns, was born on January 20th, 1896 and died on March 9th, 1996. He was full of wonderful quotes. One of my favorites is, "I always look to the future because that is where I am going to spend the rest of my life."

When interviewed in his 90s, he said that he "had to live to be 100," because he was booked at the London Palladium. He died at 100, and was a great reminder that there is a lot of life ahead of you and it is your choice as to how you spend it.

I read a great quote by author Jim Collins about the responsibility of a leader. His position is that blame should go in the mirror and credit out the window. I think what he is saying is that we succeed with the help of others and we fail as a result of our own shortcomings or lack of personal effort or diligence.

Yes, that may seem a bit harsh. Still, at the end of the day when we are brushing our teeth before bed, and when we stop blaming our parents, partners, friends, peers, bosses or whomever for our situation, we look in the mirror and we do see who is truly responsible looking back at us.

So please take charge of and care for you first.

Become your dreams and aspirations.

It will position you much better to help yourself, or take charge of, and care for, others.

TWO

VERBALIZE — if it sounds bad, chances are it is.

How often have you regretted doing something only to have someone say, "Why didn't you tell me you were thinking of that? I never would have let you do it."

I probably could have avoided most of the stupid things I have done if I had just taken a few minutes to first run the idea by someone objective.

How often do you read in the paper about foolish things that people have done or continue to do? And it doesn't have to be as extreme as being a Darwin Award winner, either.

You ask yourself, "How could they be so stupid?"

There is not a person I know that hasn't fired off an email or left a nasty voicemail, only to bemoan the fact that they hadn't bounced the content off someone else first. In all these cases, I suspect the person was egged on by their brain — the servant to our desires. Politicians, priests, neighbors, businesspeople, friends, strangers, and you and I, do equally doltish things — or worse.

I am willing to bet that if you asked yourself, or me, or anyone you know, if they discussed a dumb idea with anyone else beforehand, the answer would be no. By the way, this faux pas is not the sole providence of individuals. It happens to groups as well.

There are bad advertising ideas, ineffective policies, failed businesses, shamed coaches and clergy, adventures that went awry and, of course, countless 'trusted' officials who get caught with their fingers in our cookie jar.

So, what do we call it when people are guilty of collective stupidity?

Groupthink!

Or perhaps we should call it *Groupdidnotthink!*

Here is Wikipedia's definition of *Groupthink:* "a psychological phenomenon that occurs within a group of people in which the desire for harmony or conformity in the group results in an irrational or dysfunctional decision-making outcome."

That's a somewhat complex way of saying that the group didn't bounce its idea off anyone who wasn't committed to the same (ultimately doomed) outcome...someone that wasn't part of the group.

Bossthink is another concept I am coining right here: anyone in a leadership role needs to be wary, because most people will tend to agree with whoever is paying them or has ultimate power over them. When you consider *Bossthink*, think "the emperor has no clothes."

Why do individuals or groups become convinced by their own brains — or by each other — that some of the hurtful or illegal things they did sounded good at the time?

I have no idea, but I do have a solution.

Avoid planning alone!

The next time you or your group are conjuring up a scheme that is beyond normal, day-to-day life, for goodness' sake, run it by someone beyond your group before you run with it.

The mere act of having someone listen to your plan or read your work will expose its truth. It is amazing to me how profound this simple act is.

Words spoken out loud will echo truth that your mind's voice, in its darkness, can and often does conceal.

I am regularly amazed at how much positive evolution there can be in an idea, a letter, an email, or subject for a conversation, just through the simple act of sharing.

I regularly go to a senior colleague and have a conversation that sounds something like this. "I am going to give So And So a call right now and find out what they meant by their actions when they…" My colleague will invariably look at me like I am a lunatic because I don't have all of the facts and I am responding without time for thought. "Never mind," I nod, when I see the look. "I'll wait and get more information."

In our company, we have a policy that no email can be sent to a client in response to an issue without a third party reviewing it first. You might be surprised at the changes that are made to messages or the number of emails that don't get sent at all.

We also ensure that a second person sits in on every Human Resources meeting that involves a contentious or interpersonal issue.

It is hard to talk and listen at the same time.

Innocent ideas, poorly executed, can go very badly.

I heard a story about a male senior manager who had to let a female employee go. The plan was to ensure that she did not enter the workplace that day. Instead, she was to report to head office to arrange a meeting with the Human Resources department.

No one could reach her at home, so the senior manager decided to drive over to her workplace and meet her before she entered the front door. It must have seemed like a reasonable idea at the time.

He arrived in the parking lot a bit late.

It was raining hard.

No sooner had he stopped his car than he saw the employee making a beeline from her car to the building entrance.

He wanted to make sure his mission got accomplished, so he jumped from his car into the rain and onto the wet pavement.

"Over here," he yelled.

She looked through the downpour, paused, then ran toward him.

Out of courtesy, feeling that he couldn't just stand in the parking lot in the deluge and fire her, he invited her to get into his car.

They closed the doors. Rain pelted down on the roof.

The silence was thick. Then bad went to worse.

He decided to deliver the news to her, there and then, rather than explain that head office needed to chat with her and that he had her shift covered.

She started to cry.

He felt horrible.

He expressed his concern.

She cried harder.

He leaned over and gave her a light, encouraging hug, and then asked if she would like to get a coffee and if she would be okay to drive. Can you see a disaster in the making?

Virtually every step of his decision-making process was wrong and a potential step toward disaster.

I understand that he is no longer in management with that company. Does your stomach churn at the thought of something similar that you might have done in the past?

Even baby steps, that seemed perfect in his mind, led him down a path to potential ruin. You can easily replace that man with anyone else, in any other situation that could get critical. Can you see how a quick call to someone on the outside could help avert disaster?

So I say, "When in doubt, shout it out!"

I promise you that the second you start to share a scheme with someone, it will ring true or false as your words hit the air. Don't get me wrong. I am not trying to dumb down the adventuresome or creative problem-solving side in you and, yes, we have all had exhilarating times by winging it. It's just that I can assure you that a life filled with flying by the seat of your pants will eventually get you in trouble.

Think about something regrettable you have done that hurt someone or hurt you. Can you honestly tell me that you would have had the support of an objective friend had you called one first and told them what you were up to?

Think about a few day-to-day, common occurrences like insensitive or poorly thought-out phone calls, or email messages that we all initiate without any external guidance. We have all made an impulsive call, or pressed send, only to regret it. We have all made presentations or held meetings that went poorly because we didn't know our material well enough. We have all had a conversation with a friend or loved one that went horribly awry because we failed to test it in advance.

If you are working through something sensitive on your own, with no one around at that moment to be your sounding board, it is better to say out loud what you are about to do than to just let your brain convince you to do it.

While running through a sensitive discussion, a presentation script or speech aloud, even on your own, may seem a bit crazy, I can assure you that it leads to a far smoother delivery when the time comes.

When I edited my first book, *Critical Care*, I read the entire 600-plus pages aloud, to myself, and more than once, to hear how it sounded. I was surprised at how much I discovered and corrected.

It is extremely hard, and sometimes impossible, to edit our own thoughts or writing. Once it is written or locked in our minds, it gets harder and harder to review. If we are making a mistake, we'll make it repeatedly rather than knowing how to correct it. That is why we need impartial observers to assist us in doing, saying or writing the right thing.

Critical Care was some 180,000 words. It had been read by dozens of people, all looking for typos and grammatical errors. Before it went to press, I paid two separate English graduates to proofread it and find any more mistakes.

Even after all that, we found 42 typos in the first published version!

Beware: spell-check on your computer is not your friend and will not do your editing for you.

These principles apply to our behavior in the same way they do to our writing, thinking or talking.

When I was young and behaving badly, I just couldn't see it. I was blinded by the arrogance of self and thought what I was doing was just fine. Luckily, there were some people in my life who helped me see the errors of my ways when I couldn't. I can't say that I always wanted to hear their message, though I am sure glad now that they took the time to tell me.

Every day, we see people behaving badly. I wonder if they ever "call a friend" first.

Have you ever heard this saying about truth?

"The truth is best seen by the eye unclouded by longing."

When we are passionate about something, we are blinded by our desire, oblivious to potential pitfalls or ramifications. Being passionate about all we do is great, as long as we are not guided solely by that which we long for.

Promise me — no, promise yourself — that from today on, you will verbalize your big thoughts with someone unconnected to the outcome, before they become actions.

Hey — I want to hear you say that out loud.

THREE

MOODS — the weather vane of our soul.

Are you moody?

Do you know someone who is moody?

How do you deal with mood shifts?

We all have moods, to some degree. Some people have wide and deep mood shifts. Others have more subtle ones. When I was young, I was broody, not moody, and I suspect that was more about me seeking attention than actually responding to the world around me.

In my twenties, I would experience extreme mood shifts. I would go from being in a great mood, having a wonderful time with the company I was with, to suddenly being irritable, agitated and prone to saying incredibly hurtful things to the people around me.

After years of trying to figure this out, and spending time with people who were prone to the same erratic behaviour, I realized what the problem was: I needed to eat! Yep, that's all it took. Throw me some calories and my moods were right back up where they should be. Now I am rarely found without a snack of some sort nearby, and I recognize my hunger-related mood shifts immediately. This discovery was likely one of the most important things I ever learned about myself in terms of achieving my goals with people.

There are many triggers for mood swings, from simple things that annoy us, to fatigue or stress or pressure with peers, work, family, health or finances. And, of course, there are moods that are caused by medical conditions. I want to focus on the type of mood shifts that you and I can handle on our own without seeking a doctor's help. Seriously, though, if you find yourself in a glum mood for more than a day or two, and on a recurring basis, speak to your health professional about it.

I'm talking about the sort of stuff that, for one reason or another, gets under our skin and irritates us to the point of a short-term reaction or a downward spiral that can last a few hours or the rest of the day. Sometimes, there isn't even an identifiable cause.

Some days, I am just plain grumpy. It doesn't happen often, but it does happen. I am generally a pretty happy person. I work to find the positive in people and situations, though I have rooted in me that ability to "snap." I can have a sharp and quick tongue, so I need to be careful. My brain can generate instant responses to situations that annoy me. I try to always monitor what my mouth is about to say about what my brain is thinking. Doing this has been a great help to me, although, toss in a lack of sleep, a little hunger or low sugar, perhaps a rainy day and some pressure at work and, whoa, there's a recipe for a regrettable response to the world around me.

If this happens to you, then you know that the smallest things can become huge annoyances and have a major impact on your day, or worse, on the people you are with.

So, I came across two little bits of knowledge that have been extremely useful to me and want to share them with you.

First, when I am grumpy, I warn the people I run into that I am grumpy. No, not strangers — people like my wife and my friends or work colleagues.

I probably should warn strangers because they can get under my skin, but yelling out the window of my car, "I am grumpy," seems a bit extreme. With those close to me, I just say something like, "Before we even start talking, I need to tell you that I have a real grump on today. Nothing you did. Just want to get my mood out there."

Surprisingly, after sharing that a few times, I begin to feel better. It may be because I get empathy in return and that feels good. Maybe that's one of the cures. If I can't be open with the person I'm with, I use a different strategy called "Let the first thought pass."

Here's how it works: I have learned that my heart will always give me a better answer to an emotional question or situation than my brain will. Unfortunately, my mouth is closer to my brain than to my heart. I've learned to let the first thought from my brain kind of slip into oblivion, and wait that extra second to see what my heart has to say. In most cases, I end up saying nothing about some minute annoyance. In a second, it is over because my heart deemed it unworthy of comment.

As a newlywed, this has been particularly helpful because, as some of you may know, there can be lots of little annoyances in a relationship. I swear I can sometimes feel a wave of annoyance moving up my legs. Do you know the one I mean? I suspect you do!

Thus, as a neophyte husband, I ask myself two questions: 1) How important is this? 2) Is this the right time?

I bet you can guess what happens next. In those few extra seconds, letting my heart combat my brain, the heart always wins. If I listen to it, I hear the answers: 1) not very and 2) no.

I let it go and move on. The problem is solved, because there was no real problem in the first place. It was just a mood causing me to react.

What I have learned most about "off" moods is to listen to them and try to understand the source. I actually have little conversations with my moods, so they know that I am wise to them.

"Yes, yes," I will think. "Hey, thanks for those negative thoughts on this rainy day, buddy."

You know what? My mood begins to improve. After all, what is a mood but something we generate within ourselves? Why shouldn't we be able to control it, or at least understand it?

Another strategy I find helpful is reflecting back on other times when I felt that same mood, trying to remember and understand what brought it on and what I did about it at that time. One thing I know: good moods precede off moods, and off moods precede good moods. I am not aware of any well-functioning person who is happy all the time or moody all the time. As humans, I feel that we do need to know some downs if we are to appreciate the ups.

Over the years, I have discovered truths about my moods by listening to them as they work their way through me. I ask questions of myself as to why I feel, or have felt, a certain way. Understanding them, even talking to them, led me to action and action helped, as it usually does.

I like lots of light and sunshine, so dark, dull, gray days can drag me down. Now I keep my office very brightly lit while I work, and that has had a tremendous positive impact on my outlook.

I need eight or more hours of sleep; when I am sleep deprived, I am moodier.

I need quiet time and I seek it regularly.

I get annoyed in big crowds, so I prepare myself mentally before I'm exposed to one.

I am a buyer, not a shopper, so I avoid spending time with people who like to poke along and browse for hours.

My wife is very creative and likes to scour stores and look at lots of different items. She often invites me to come. I usually decline. Because she understands me, she is considerate about my aversion. I once gave her a gift certificate that promised I would spend two hours shopping with her. She was very appreciative, because she knew how hard that would be for me.

I enjoy a fast pace in life, so I am careful now to avoid situations that are tedious or slow unless, of course, I want silence!

I find heavy commuter traffic and traffic chaos to be a huge waste of time, life and spirit, so I avoid highways and congested areas wherever possible. I admire people who make the sacrifice of a long commute each day to provide for their family. If only we could figure out a better way and give people that time back.

To be candid, that's why I fly. Actually, I decided to get my pilot's licence when I got engaged. My wife's family lives in a town that's five hours away and requires driving through a large metropolitan area. I knew that I'd be eating a bitter pill on every trip, so I hit the books and became a pilot. It wasn't easy, but it was the best way I could see it working out. Now we can rise early, fly to her family home, and be sitting in church with her parents on a Sunday morning.

Moods are signaling us that something isn't quite right. Much like a headache or tummy ache, moods are like a spirit ache. Pay attention to them, learn from them and create choices that minimize the impact they can have on a day, or worse, a relationship.

Moods can be a challenge, for sure, and it is always best to avoid extremes to try and manage them. But we can all try hard to avoid letting moods govern our days. Acknowledge them, think about them, talk to them, just don't give in to them. Use positive internal talk and remind yourself that "this too shall pass." Hey, you can also wear one of the "Keep Calm and Carry On" T-shirts as a great visual cue.

This is not to say that one wants to be a moodless, bland, vanilla drone. On the contrary, our moods are the waves of our internal ocean. We just need to learn how to surf them and not get washed up on the shore by them.

You can start tuning in to your moods today.

What makes you happy, angry, annoyed, sad, aggressive or pensive?

How long do the moods last?

What worked, or didn't work, to change your mood?

Physical, visual and audio cues can have a huge impact on my mood and I have learned what works and what doesn't.

For instance, being close to water and having a view of the water is likely second only to sunshine in terms of physical indicators that make me feel happy.

What sights, sounds and physical things elevate your mood?

How can you bring more of that into your life?

If you really want to understand your moods, just start tuning in now. Moods, like the little bird that you will read about herein that is always talking, may just be trying to tell you something.

Are you listening or reacting to your moods? The choice is yours to make and manage them.

FOUR

CONVERSATION — the one you are most resisting.

How often have you awakened in the middle of the night recently, thinking about someone you need to have a “difficult” conversation with?

How long have you been putting it off?

How many times a day or week do you think about it?

Is it someone you see at work each day?

Is it a friend that you socialize with?

Is it someone you love and are afraid to confront or hurt?

Is it someone from your past that you would just like to rebuild a bridge with?

Guess what? These difficult conversations are something we all need to have occasionally.

The funny thing is that, much like the truth, they will surface eventually. Like it or not, you will have the conversation. The trouble is that if you wait until the matter boils over, you won’t have control of the timing, the place or the most important thing — the outcome.

Don’t wait.

The most difficult conversation, the one you are most resisting, is the one you need to have the soonest.

Is your stomach churning at the mere thought of it?

Are your palms sweating?

That's okay.

It's fine to be nervous about a difficult conversation. It shows that you care about the outcome.

You are waking up in the middle of the night because during the day you can consciously suppress things that are bothering you. At night, though, your guard is down. Your subconscious takes over and digs up anything you've tried to bury.

Sometimes that's a good thing. A very good thing. How often do you wake up with a solution to a problem that plagued you all day? How often does the location of something you were looking for just pop into your mind in the middle of the night? Pretty cool, the way the brain works.

That's your inner smart self! That little bird that knows the right answer.

You need to listen to it and act on things that dawn at night.

We already know the difficult conversations we need to have. I have learned to just get on with them.

I picture such a conversation and, most importantly, I try to pick a time of day and location that are good for both parties. Neutral space, if you will. Trapping someone in an uncomfortable place just adds pressure to the moment.

My father always chose to have difficult conversations with me in the car. There were few words that brought more fear to my soul than, "Let's go for a drive."

"Why?" I would ask. "I don't want to go for a drive."

"Go get in the car," he would answer.

Uh oh. Something was up. Usually something he had found out about my comings and goings that he was less than impressed with. I suggest that you don't have difficult conversations in a car — especially if it is moving!

There are difficult conversations that need to be had in work-related and personal situations. Try to have these conversations somewhere private and plan enough time to give all parties a chance to listen carefully, ask questions, let it soak in and, ideally, respond.

If it is about work and you are a subordinate, you will need to book a meeting with the appropriate person. You will likely have to explain what you want to talk about and how much time you need. You'll want to make it clear that you can meet when it's most convenient for them.

In that situation, it's wise to take in a piece of paper or a notepad with your talking points on it. Be brief. Stick to your notes. Keep the emotion at bay while you express how important the issue is to you.

Be prepared for your superior to ask for time to reflect and don't be surprised if they wish to bring someone into the meeting with them to take notes. In today's hypersensitive workplaces, few managers will meet one-on-one to explore difficult issues with employees.

You need to know what your boundaries and options are before you engage in the conversation. Think ahead about the likely responses, how you will feel about each one and, more importantly, what you will do in each case.

You are the CEO of YOU Inc., so take charge of your issues and be proactive. Suffering in silence will cause you far more harm in the long run than dealing directly and reasonably with issues at hand.

Difficult conversations with friends or loved ones are the hardest because they generally deal with matters of the heart, not the head. You have to know what you want to talk about and be prepared for any and all outcomes. The location you choose can have a big impact on how the talk goes.

I prefer to be outdoors, walking along a path or stream, when I try to tackle one of these tough personal conversations. If the weather is foul, I find that the living or dining room is the next best choice — never the bedroom with a partner.

Ask when the other person might be available and give an idea of what is coming.

"When would it be convenient to get some time with you to talk about something that's been on my mind about …?" It could be anything — your future, a situation, finance, love life, health — but, whatever it is, give them a heads-up.

Too often, people just blurt something out and hit someone between the eyes with a difficult topic, and in an appropriate place, to boot. This concept is about mending bridges, not throwing someone off one.

Always have difficult conversations privately, away from other people and — above all — away from your children.

Always have difficult conversations with a clear head and never when either or both of you are under the influence of booze or drugs.

Always make certain that the other party has the required time to listen, reflect and respond. Make sure they don't have another obligation looming that may cut short the conversation.

Yes, some of this may seem obvious, but think about how many people you know who have brought difficult topics up over lunch or a dinner out, while on vacation, at parties or over the phone or email.

By the way, here are two more "always": Always try to resolve issues of the heart face to face and always avoid email, text or social media channels for such important conversations. Remember this saying: "Eighty percent of success is just showing up."

I have found it incredible how much of an issue dissolves away when I am face to face with someone I care about and am open to the outcome of our chat.

So, make a decision soon to get on with one of those difficult conversations. In fact, there's no time like right now to book one. If you have several to tackle, I suggest you pick the easiest one first for a bit of practice.

Be patient. It may take weeks or months before you're at a point where you have caught up with all of those long-deferred conversations. I hope you only have one or two on your mind, but for some, there will be deep-rooted, long-standing matters that will take time to work through.

One conversation with someone won't necessarily resolve everything. I can assure you, though, that if you stick with this concept and follow through, you will see the benefits.

You may be scared. You may cry or laugh, but please remember to stay calm.

Your heart will be lighter the moment you begin.

You will be rewarded with the love that can flow between two people when they face difficult interpersonal issues and resolve to make them better.

Having the difficult conversation will likely reveal the truth of the relationship and set the course for the future. It may not always be the course you want to be on, but it is the course you most likely need to be on.

So, who are you about to reach out to?

You can consciously decide now…or your brain will talk to you at 3 a.m.

FIVE

BIRD — your wise inner voice.

How often has something gone wrong in your life and the first thing you said was, "I knew that was going to happen!"

We all have a little inner "bird" that is continually tweeting messages to us to help guide our journey by providing some guidance and guardrails along life's road. In some cases, that little bird can dramatically change, or even save, your life. Sometimes the messages are simple and joyous, sometimes profound.

This year, we made a nice skating rink in front of the house. It didn't get used too much, but the act of creating it was quite joyful and serene. One day, after work, I was flooding the rink. The sun was setting and the air was crackling with that familiar evening chill of late winter. The sound of the water spraying from the hose had a mesmerizing effect on me. Darkness was setting in and I wondered how the ice would be in the morning.

My friend, his son, his son's pal and I had ripped up and down the rink most of the previous afternoon. The rink was such a hit, my buddy and I started making plans for next year's. The rum and Cokes we were sipping helped us visualize how much grander that rink would be.

My friend had returned to the rink with the kids, while I had tramped through the snow, in my skates, to my deck, a couple of hundred feet away.

There is something special about the feeling of tired and squeezed feet being pulled out of skates. I remember loving that release as a kid and it hasn't changed in my adulthood.

The wind was calm and the trees were still when I heard a chirp in the air. For a moment, I thought it was a squirrel.

Then another chirp replied.

Then several more. Back and forth they called.

The scuffle of skates on the rink was the only other sound.

The chirping continued.

"It's birds," I thought. "Spring is almost here."

I couldn't see them, but I knew they could see me.

I wondered if they were being entertained by the activity on the rink.

I sat still on the steps and listened to their song as they chatted back and forth, sending out a hopeful message to eavesdroppers.

It made me smile and be thankful. Spring was approaching even though, to the naked eye, it still seemed a lot like winter.

As I enjoyed that moment, I thought about the many messages that come to me unbidden — messages that just seem to fly into my mind and offer me guidance, if I listen to them.

The wooden steps I was sitting on reminded me of the stairs that led down into the basement of the farmhouse where I lived when I was a boy. My earliest memory of my little inner bird speaking to me happened at the bottom of those rickety stairs.

The basement had a concrete floor that my dad had painted gray. My dad loved to apply paint to surfaces.

Thick wooden beams and rounded posts held up the limestone house. Above me rose two modest stories. The basement seemed cavernous to me at the age of five. I know now that it wasn't more than six feet in height and measured only about forty feet by forty feet.

I remember my dad sitting at the bottom of the basement stairs each morning, polishing his black shoes with a brush. When he buffed them with a polishing cloth, he could make it snap as he whipped it across the leather tips. Those sounds were a subliminal message about work ethic, pride and appearance.

I loved playing at the bottom of those basement stairs.

There, it felt like I was a long way from home even though I could still hear the noises and smell my mother's cooking in the kitchen.

"Phillip?" she would call. "Stay at the bottom of the stairs and be careful."

"Okay," I would call back, innocently, as I hacked away at something with one of the good kitchen knives I had smuggled down under my shirt.

Thinking back, with one fall I would have impaled myself.

Even at that young age, I knew instinctively that I was doing something wrong. Perhaps the fact that I was so close to the kitchen and my mom made it seem like it was okay.

Bad things rarely happen as a result of one bad decision. A series of bad decisions usually culminate in a bad thing. So many wrongs: I took the knife; I hid it under my shirt; I hiked down the stairs; I was hacking away at one of my brother's wooden toys...yet I feigned innocence when my mom called down to me.

I can still clearly recall the moment.

Long, sawing motions with the good knife.

Something in my mind chirping, "This is not going to turn out well, Phillip."

I lost focus and drew the blade across the back of my thumb.

The smooth, silent, painless slice of metal through skin resulted. The pause, as I observed the white flap peel open.

A beat.

The world was silent.

Then a gush of blood accompanied by its best friend: searing pain.

My ears rang.

My eyes went blurry.

My mouth opened and out came a scream that likely sent a dagger through my mother's heart.

That was the day, so many years ago at the bottom of the farmhouse basement steps, I first learned about The Bird.

We all have one. The bird is our protector, our subconscious. It is wise. It knows us better than we will ever know ourselves and it always knows the future. It is a stalwart and ever-present companion that will never let us down, no matter how many times we doubt or ignore it. The bird knows every answer to every question about our life or circumstances. If the bird doesn't know, it will pose a question that will lead us to the answer.

The bird is a quiet orator of truth that avoids competing with the cacophony of noise that we immerse our beings in. It is up to us to tune in and listen; to get quiet for a while and hear the bird's wisdom.

The interesting thing about the bird is that the more complex one's situation is, the wiser the bird becomes.

Of course, the bird's answers are usually pretty simple. The one I most often hear these days is, "Hmmm...I wouldn't do that if I were you."

Great success, I have been told, is built more upon what one does not do than what one does in life.

Think back.

How many times has your inner bird cautioned, "Hmmm...I wouldn't do that if I were you."

Did you listen to the bird or ignore it?

If you ignored it, how did that work out for you?

Your inner bird is wise, but only helpful if you heed it.

Nowadays, when life throws me a curve, I try to step back and assess whether I may be heading in the wrong direction. I ask myself, "Is it just the signal I need to change course, ease off or try a new approach?"

It has been to my disadvantage every time I have ignored my inner wise bird. I often used to resent the bird's messages. Now I embrace them.

I often think that the person who first said, "Hindsight is 20/20," had ignored his or hers, and paid a price.

Your wise inner bird is a forward thinker. From its perch on high, it can see sooner what you will ultimately see.

The beautiful thing is that the bird is also a teacher. If you tune in and listen, it willingly shares its secrets with you. Just listen and ask why it is sending you a message, and you will become wiser. I've often reflected that the words "why" and "wiser" sound similar for a reason. It seems the more we ask why, the wiser we may become.

Tune in and pay attention to your inner bird. You may just be surprised to discover that the answers you seek are already within.

SIX

VISUALIZE — if you can see it, you can be it.

What did you think about when you got up this morning and looked in the mirror?

How did you see your day playing out?

What did you see when you thought about your partner, your children or your peers at work or play?

How often has something happened in your life and you thought, "I knew that was going to happen," or, "I could see that coming a mile away."

Would you believe me if I told you that you have the power to see the future?

Well, you do!

I don't mean predicting winning lottery numbers or stocks. I mean that you have the power to influence yourself and those around you to trend toward a certain outcome.

That's why I like the saying, "If you can see it, you can be it."

When you listen to successful people talk about their achievements, they will usually say things like, "I have always seen myself becoming this leader (or singer or actor or parent…)."

Conversely, some people see themselves in a negative way and follow their parents, peers or others in a negative direction.

The power of visualizing success for others can have a major effect on those who look up to you as a parent, coach, manager, friend or colleague. If you continually support people and help them see themselves in the winning way you see them, it will help them visualize success. Of course, the reverse is true as well if you tell or show them you see them in an unfavorable light.

In a leadership role, your vision can become theirs.

I had a wonderful friend named Herb. He was an awesome man and had the ability to help you see the great qualities in yourself, which were often hidden. When Herb passed away, I was unable to attend his funeral so I later watched a recording of the service. One of the speakers said, "Many of you may not have known this, but Herb had a lifelong condition of double vision."

I was completely caught off guard by that statement. I had known Herb for many years and considered him a close friend. I couldn't understand how it was that I didn't know that. Apparently, I wasn't the only person who was surprised; a murmur ran through the crowd.

Herb was a guy with a big personality. He had played major leadership roles in his life. He hadn't even worn glasses. I think we all wondered what the heck the speaker was talking about until he continued.

"Yes, that's right, Herb had double vision. Whenever he spoke to you, he saw two people. He saw who you were at that moment and he also saw who you were capable of being and the latter is the person he always spoke to."

Those who had gathered to celebrate Herb's life then knew exactly what the speaker saying. A ripple of smiles, nods and appreciative chuckles passed through the room.

As I recognized the powerful truth the speaker had revealed, several encounters with Herb flashed through my mind. Every conversation I had ever had with Herb left me feeling like I could conquer any goal.

Visualization is a constant process that we engage in every waking second. It also flows into our sleep and dreams. The challenge is to make it an active, as well as passive, process.

Typically, we passively let our mind send images to us about how things will play out. I found that in the absence of my involvement in that process, my mind typically sent me negative or worst-case scenarios.

I was lucky to have been a successful, competitive athlete who received training in sports at a young age. That training included seeing a successful conclusion to what I was trying to accomplish. It took me many years, though, to bring that visualization process into the rest of my life.

I wish I could tell you how it all started or that it was a very deliberate and conscious process. Truthfully, though, I have to admit that I just sort of stumbled into it bit by bit through reading, taking courses, or in conversation with people like Herb.

If you are practiced at visualization, you are likely well on your way to achieving your goals, living well, or at least working towards both.

If this is new to you, though, the first thing I recommend is that you start to tune into the pictures and images your brain is sending to you about all the various aspects of your life. There is no trick to this. The second you tell yourself that you want to access the pictures, they will come.

Over the next few days or weeks, you will very quickly grasp whether you are full of negative, neutral or positive visions of yourself, other people and the world around you.

One technical step to this process, that you may find helpful, is to write down the big categories in your life — such as health, family or peer relations, work, community, fitness, finance, home life, hobbies, sleep and other important categories — that you want to achieve short- and long-term success in. Your list will be your unique list. It may be long or short to start, but I can guarantee that it will grow as you become hooked on positive visualization.

Beside each category, write out an objective or two that describes the outcome you wish for it and when you hope to achieve that outcome. Here's an example:

Family – eat one meal together each day (1 week); make amends with my sister (1 month); set some boundaries around kids and technology (2 weeks); improve communication within our family (3 months).

Now you can make this a positive verbal and visual affirmation to focus on, through creating a sentence that adds emotion and importance:

"I see my family having fun and learning more about each other by eating one meal together each day, starting within one week."

"I see the positive outcome that will happen when I make amends with my sister this month."

"I see the positive benefit from the extra time I will get with my children by setting some boundaries, in the next two weeks, around their use of technology at home."

"My family will argue less and know and care for each other more as we continue to improve the communication between us over the next three months."

The beautiful thing about this is that your mind has infinite capacity for visualizing and you have the power to make every vision a positive one.

Initially, you will feel like you are playing mental ping-pong as you see a negative vision, convert it to something positive, and send it back into your mind.

I will let you in on a little secret I now know: this process is lifelong. It is like a muscle that needs continuous exercise or it will wither. Some days, you will find it hard to be positive, so just go through the mental, mechanical exercise. When you are tired or sick, it will be harder. When someone treats you poorly, it will be harder. When something awful happens to you or someone you care about, it will be really hard.

You must persevere and you will see and be rewarded with the benefit, even on those darkest days of your life.

No, visualization is not a perfect science or art. If you believe that we tend to be guided to where we should be going, rather than where we think we want to be going, this admission of mine will resonate with you.

During my years as an amateur stage actor, I had pretty good success and ended up playing lead roles in our community-theater productions. We always had receptive houses and I generally received good reviews. I went to Toronto and New York regularly to see plays and visualized myself on those larger stages one day. I truly loved the acting world. If you ask me today what my dream job would be, I would still say to be a Broadway actor.

I was sitting with Herb at a restaurant in the Thousand Islands in Canada a few years after my father had died. I had immersed myself in writing and acting, possibly because my father had never supported my desire to be in the arts. Now, in his absence, I had the chance. After a long and enjoyable meal talking about my acting aspirations, Herb said, "Phillip, one day you will be on Broadway." He was incredibly inspirational and I took his statement to heart. I knew he meant that if I wanted it badly enough and kept a positive vision, I would get there.

Flash forward a number of years and there I was at the opening of the Broadway play production of the famous book *Tuesdays With Morrie.*

It was a cool Tuesday on the 19th of November 2002.

The house was full. The theater buzzed with anticipation. I could feel my nerves tingling from my head to my toes.

The lights dimmed.

The audience fell silent. You could have heard the proverbial pin drop.

The curtain rose.

Mitch or Morrie — I can't remember — stepped into the light and the play began.

No, I wasn't onstage. I was one of the financial supporters of the production and I had a great seat. I smiled, thinking about Herb's prophetic words, "Phillip, one day you will be on Broadway." And so I was; just not exactly as I had envisioned it!

You see, we have to have a little bit of give in our vision as well, because the universe can't always give us exactly what we think we want. It can come close, though. Visualizing has certainly guided me well thus far.

I am sure that you have heard the saying about being careful what you wish for because it just might come true. I believe those are insightful words indeed.

Many have written about the power of positive thought and visualization and the direct relationship both have on outcomes. To me, one thing is for certain: the more use I make of visualization, the more rewarding and better my life continues to become.

So, going forward, I ask you to give it a try. There is no downside. It's really not that hard. Tuning in to the movie that is playing in your head is fun, actually, as well as beneficial.

Oh, by the way, once you start playing that reel, you can't stop.

You will probably also find that positive visualization, just before you fall asleep, even has positive impacts on your dreams and restfulness.

So, start small and start now. See the positive outcome in whatever is important to you, and become it.

Wait — you don't have any choice in the matter, because I am visualizing for you the health, happiness, contentment and success you will have when you begin, right now, to turn your desires into positive images in your mind and deflect the negative images that are holding you back.

SEVEN

SMART AND RIGHT — do what's right even when no one is looking.

"Hey, that's two words!"

I know. Bear with me.

Have you ever done something really clever that, in the end, upset one or more people?

Have you ever taken a position on a matter where the facts were undeniably on your side, but in the end upset one or more people?

Keep reading and these two words will become the best "word," and maybe the only word, you need to lead a life of joy, full of sustainable success.

It is "integrity," wrapped in two simple words.

Smart and right represent the moral dilemma that we often face as opportunities to cheat or take a shortcut tempt us.

I am sure we have all been disappointed with revelations about one of our heroes from sports, politics, business, Hollywood, the clergy or just plain life.

At a very young age, we all stumble across things that make us smart, or at least seem smart.

We find out where Mom and Dad keep some money. We find out where the car keys are. We find out how to get into the liquor cabinet. We find out that by threatening someone, we can get them to do something for us or keep a secret. We find out there's a hole we can look through and see something we shouldn't. We find out that teasing someone can make them cry. We find out that dressing a certain way, acting a certain way, or having certain things can make us seem popular. We find out we can read the smart kid's test answers over her shoulder. We find out that we can hand in someone else's work as our own.

But then we get caught and we are embarrassed or, worse, punished and told that what we were doing was wrong. Suddenly we don't feel so smart.

For some, that's all it takes. "Once caught, never forgot." For others, the pattern continues and the smart acts get more serious, as do the consequences.

The sooner we can learn or teach others that smart actions need to be balanced with the right purpose, the better we or that person can be.

It is so easy to live in lies. It is easy to take the shortcut, or say or do what's needed in the moment, rather than what was right for the long term.

Succumbing to our weakness for temptation seems universal. We see it at all levels of society, from the rich to the poor and from the weak to the most powerful or revered people on the planet.

We see them doing wrong things because they were smart enough to find a loophole or think that they wouldn't get caught. We see them doing or saying ridiculous things in the name of some "right" principal.

How do we get to a place where we do what's smart only when it is right, and we do what's right only when it's smart?

How do we do what's right when no one is looking, or live in such a way that our actions and behaviors would look good on the front page of the newspaper?

I am sure that we have all met very bright people who continually aggravate us with their knowledge. But, while they are smart, they use their smarts to put others down.

What's the point of cleverly figuring out someone's computer password only to get caught and lose a good friend or, worse, hurt someone because your actions are wrong?

Who loses if you decide that certain bit of knowledge will allow you to take something that isn't yours?

How does it build a loving relationship if you are snooping in your partner's emails or social media account?

Thanks to the discipline doled out by my father and his many lectures about being a good boy, I count myself lucky to have had several powerful events that taught me the valuable lesson I am writing about and try to live by each day.

A female friend of mine had returned from a lengthy overseas trip. I had been concerned and perhaps a bit jealous in her absence. I was seeking assurances that those feelings were unfounded.

One evening, I noticed her diary open on a side table. Pages full of writing were clearly visible. I knew better than to look, so I ignored it…for a while. It seemed that every step I took in the house on that one particular evening led me past that table. The urge to pick up the diary was powerful. I could feel it coursing through my body.

I resisted and did not pick up the book, but I had glanced down at it a couple of times and these few words had leapt off the page: "I miss James so much and love him with all my heart."

I was sickened by that revelation, but I was even more sickened by the fact that I had let myself see it. Days and sleepless nights ensued. I provoked no confrontation. I just suffered in silence. Then the moment of truth finally came, as I knew it would.

Candles were lit, dinner was served, and wine was flowing.

"I want to share one of the most powerful things about my trip with you, Phillip," she said in the nonchalant way an executioner deftly lifts an ax. "I was volunteering at an orphanage…"

"Here it comes," I thought. "She's hooked up with some expatriate volunteer do-gooder."

"… and I fell head over heels in love with this little orphaned boy named James…"

"I'm such an idiot," I thought.

"He's only three and he has the biggest brown eyes and the brightest smile and…"

I couldn't hear any more. My ears were ringing, my heart was pounding, my chest felt heavy, and my stomach ached. "Sorry, what did you say?" I managed.

"I decided to become his sponsor," she continued earnestly. "It only costs a few dollars a month, but that money goes so far over there…"

I later went to Africa and met little James. He was indeed a joy. As I looked down into his eyes, I thought, "Thank you, James. From the least likely place on earth came the most powerful of lessons."

I was 35 when I spent those seven months in Africa. I learned many things and met many people there but, most importantly, I met me and learned about myself. I learned what it took to be, and live, right and smart.

I remember taking a water taxi from the main village of Lamu Island in Kenya to another village, Shella, where we were staying. During that 20-minute boat ride, I came to realize that I was then and forever blessed with new knowledge that could change my life.

I realized that I was no longer capable of knowingly committing insensitive acts. That was not to say that I wouldn't make mistakes — of course I would say or do some stupid things in the future. The difference was that I was now my own judge of right and wrong, wherever I was, whatever I was doing, even if I was alone. There was no ignoring that fact or turning away from enlightenment.

It was an awesome, but scary, feeling to know that I couldn't bullshit myself anymore and get away with it. "Sorry, I didn't realize," just wouldn't cut it anymore.

That theory was regularly tested, although never as poignantly as when I was on a conference call in Canada a few years later. It was an important call as I was making financial arrangements for a significant transaction. My lawyer, at the time, had arranged the call to introduce me to a very successful person who might have been able to help me.

The call was going along well as we made small talk and exchanged some background information about the project and each other. This was early in the cell phone days. I was holding one of those one-pound "brick" phones, as we used to call them. I was also driving, because you could talk and drive back then.

"Phillip? Phillip?" my lawyer checked.

"Yep, I'm here."

"Phillip, can you hear us?" inquired the other party.

I could clearly hear the next two comments they exchanged about cell phone reliability.

"Hey guys, I'm here," I told them. "Can you hear me?"

Clearly they could not.

Then a moment of learning or testing — depending how you see it — presented itself.

"Well, I guess we lost him," my lawyer sighed. "Why don't I take some time to tell you about Phillip Brown and his family…?"

What would you do?

What do you think I did? I will keep you in suspense and tell you at the end of this chapter.

Do what's right and what's smart, always. Reflect on challenging times or situations you've had and I bet that that message will be clear in hindsight.

Remember: Being clever or smart does not give you a license to do harmful, hurtful or illegal things.

Knowing something that others don't know does not give you the right to embarrass, belittle or cheat them. In the end, you will be bitten by breaking this simple rule, or rewarded for living by it.

The songwriter David Gates and band called Bread performed a song called Diary that captures the whole dilemma of right and smart, beautifully. Give it a listen sometime and perhaps learn, as I did, that I never really understood what he was talking about until I awoke to the concept of smart and right.

Here is a little test that I feel exemplifies the concept. I guarantee, if you try the scenario on any friend, a lively discussion will ensue.

Imagine that you have been selected to participate in a highly advertised coin-toss contest with one person. The winner gets $100,000. You are both flown to an exotic place and treated like celebrities because this whole event is being televised.

The hour arrives and you are escorted into the arena, where thousands of people wait to watch this world exclusive. You meet your fellow competitor for the first time, and it is decided that you will toss the coin and the other will call it. One flip, heads or tails, all or nothing.

The anticipation is so thick you could cut the air.

You face your competition.

Both of you are perspiring heavily.

You have dreamt over and over about what you would do with the winnings.

The emcee holds up a big coin as she walks toward you.

"Good evening, ladies and gentlemen," she says into her microphone. "Welcome to the invisible coin toss that will test the integrity of our contestants in this winner-take-all event."

"'Invisible' coin toss?" you wonder.

"Only the person who tosses the coin will know the truth and we will accept whatever answer he presents to us. We trust him to be truthful."

A murmur runs through the crowd. You are slightly dazed.

"Ladies and gentlemen, tonight we will do a coin toss for $100,000 — with no coin."

The crowd goes wild.

"The selected contestant will toss an invisible coin. He will catch the invisible coin and flip it over on the back of his hand. He will then look under his hand and determine in his mind if it is heads or tails. The caller will call and the coin-tosser will reveal whether the caller is right or wrong.

"Are you ready?" she asks you.

"Yes."

"Are you ready?" she asks the caller.

"I am."

Both of you are shaking.

The crowd noise is deafening.

The announcer looks at you.

"Toss the invisible coin high in the air, please, and catch it so no one can see the head or tail. Flip it quickly onto the back of your hand, as you would with a real coin. Decide in your mind whether it is heads or tails and ask your competitor to call it."

You can't believe what you are hearing, but there is no turning back.

The crowd is now wildly yelling, "Toss, toss, toss, toss…"

You bend your knees and, with a mighty hurl, you send the invisible coin high in the air.

The crowd screams its approval.

"Heads, heads, heads, heads!" or, "Tails, tails, tails!" they chant.

You catch it and flip it onto the back of your hand.

You peek beneath your covering hand as if there were a coin there.

"Is it heads or tails?" the emcee asks.

You decide it's heads, and lock down that thought.

"Caller, for $100,000, what do you call: heads or tails?"

The crowd is frantic, coaching your opponent on.

The caller looks at you, then back at the emcee.

"I call heads."

The crowd goes wild. The announcer waves for silence and turns to you. "For $100,000, what side of the invisible coin is up?"

You pause and soak in the moment that you know will never come again. There is a microphone in your face, cameras blazing all around you, and thousands of people have just fallen silent, waiting to hear you tell them something only you know.

You swallow hard, lift your hand as though to reveal a real coin beneath it, and announce, "It's ..."

What would you announce? Doing what's right when no one is looking, or when you have a chance to cheat a stranger, friend or a system, is a true test of integrity.

Just because you are right doesn't make you smart, and just because you are smart doesn't make you right. The two go hand in hand.

Make "right" and "smart" your partners in good decision-making and never give up either one for the other in the process.

Do what's right when no one is looking; live in such a way that your actions would play well on the front page of any local newspaper.

Now, about that conference call I mentioned earlier.

I hung up.

EIGHT

MOUTH — a road map to your health.

This is going to sound weird.

I want you to start paying attention to the taste, color, condition, acidity, sweetness, tenderness, inflammation and moisture content in your mouth.

I did and it changed my entire approach to health management.

You know those muscle aches and pains or headaches or allergies or other ailments you have? Have you ever tried connecting the condition of your mouth to how the rest of your body feels?

Years ago, I was at the hospital with an ailment. The doctor decided to do a routine physical. He asked me to remove all of my clothes and lie on my back on the cold examination table. He didn't even offer me a gown. So there I was, stark naked, as he gave me the once-over, so to speak.

"Open your mouth. Good. Stick out your tongue. Way out, now say…Wow, you have geographic tongue!" he exclaimed.

Geographic tongue? Sure, I've traveled, but I usually buy maps.

"Just a minute," he said. "I will be right back. Keep your tongue out."

There I am, naked and vulnerable, with my tongue sticking out.

"I have a group of interns in the hall. Would you mind if they came in and had a look at your tongue?"

Just for fun, readers, stick out your tongue and try to say, "Sure, no problem."

"Ladies, come in and have a look at this," I heard the doctor say.

Before this 20-something party boy could pull in his tongue — or anything else — about a dozen attractive, young, female interns gathered around me on the table and peered down into my mouth. The doctor held my tongue in place with a piece of gauze so I couldn't retract it, while he explained to them what a geographic tongue is.

I wanted to crawl into a hole. My face was crimson; on fire, really. However, I take some comfort in knowing that, somewhere out there, thanks to me, there are 12 female doctors with a keen insight into geographic tongues. It's a completely benign and not all that uncommon condition in which, basically, your tongue does appear to be sporting a map of some sort. I think mine resembled Italy.

For the next couple of evenings on the town, I prayed that I would not be recognized by any pretty interns at one of the local hot spots.

Even though my case was very mild, from that day on, I paid attention to my mouth and tongue and, surely enough, connections to my overall health appeared.

It turned out that certain acidic foods, such as tomatoes, made my tongue sensitive. That issue was easily solved, and since then my tongue has pretty much looked like — well — a tongue, rather than a foreign country.

I saw that I would get some little sores on my lips or gums several days, or even a week, before getting a cold.

I noticed that my gums were red and bled when I brushed my teeth. This led me to discover that I had early signs of gum disease. That got me flossing and using a Water Pik®, so I avoided what could have been a more serious issue.

When I am well rested and healthy, my mouth is clear, moist and clean when I awake. When I get run down, eat or drink the wrong foods or beverages, or am getting sick, my mouth tells me by its taste, stickiness or by the little sores that can appear. If I tune in and take immediate corrective action — usually by catching up on my sleep — it is quite interesting how quickly my mouth gets back to normal.

The other thing I have found, through sharing this information, is that lots of my friends have oral symptoms, but have never related them to anything beyond their mouth. They shrugged off the issue as being isolated within their mouth, rather than being a signal from another part of their body.

I actually keep a bit of an oral toolkit now to make sure I'm keeping my mouth clean and healthy. One of the best tools I have is a 5x magnifying mirror with a light on it.

This is mounted on the wall in my bathroom and it gives me an awesome view into the old oral canyon. Let me warn you, though, that there are a lot of things in and around your face that do not look pretty when well lit and magnified, but you will get used to that.

How often do you wake up in the morning and discover a piece of food in your mouth or between your teeth from the meal you had last night?

Not good, right? It has been cooking in there for eight or ten hours at nearly 100 degrees Fahrenheit! When you think of it that way, we should all be big fans of oral hygiene.

In short, watch your mouth. My regimen includes soft, un-waxed dental floss, a Water Pik®, a good quality electric toothbrush that I change the end on monthly (even though they are costly), a single-tufted brush to clean around those corners the toothbrush doesn't get, and one of those gold-handled doodads with the rubber tip on the end. When I travel, I keep a pack of Stimudents® on hand in case something gets stuck in there.

You may be very surprised at just how much goo there is in your mouth and on your teeth.

If you have never been to one, I suggest a visit to a periodontist for a lesson on oral health and hazards. The money is well spent. It's an investment that will pay dividends for life.

Your mouth, as it happens, is also that great gateway for the precious air you breathe in and out, as in out-and-in someone's face! They'll appreciate your clean mouth because it leads to clean breath — unless you've just scarfed down a chicken and bean burrito, in which case I can't help you.

I know some of you may be thinking, what about my nose? The truth is that most of us breathe through our mouths.

Have you ever actually thought about, or focused on, your breathing?

Breathing life in is such a simple, yet forgotten or overlooked, gift.

I remember running in many road races and exerting myself so much that the tubes in my ears would open and it would feel like I was breathing through them. While it drove me a bit nuts, I knew that it was sign that I was "going for it."

I don't expect all of you to exert yourself to that degree. My point is that you and your breath are inseparable and you should get to know each other better, if you haven't already.

Is it quiet where you are now?

If not, go somewhere where it is quiet. Now, let's do something together.

Okay, close the book.

WAIT! Read what's next, and then close the book. Once the book is closed, just become aware of your nose, mouth, chest, tummy and lungs and take in a long, easy, deep, reasonably quiet lungful of air.

Pull it in through your mouth.

Hear it and feel it go in.

Hold it.

Now, release. Let it out.

Maybe this is new to you or maybe not, but c'mon, you have to admit that it's pretty darn cool.

On average, you take about 12 breaths a minute. An athlete under exertion can take over 60 breaths a minute.

For your entire life, every five seconds or so, you rely on this automatic and necessary mechanism. You can live without just about everything, except precious air.

Now, off to the bathroom you go. Open wide and take a big breath in and let it out while you watch the magic of the mechanics that give you life. Take a good look in and around your yap and see how the road map to your health really looks.

NINE

CASH — the numbers never lie.

You and your finances have a meeting coming up. Are you ready for that meeting?

Your finances are always ready to meet with you.

If you haven't read any books by the Savings Meister himself, David Chilton, then keep reading. If you have — keep reading, anyway!

How often have you had an unpleasant surprise where you discovered you didn't have quite as much money as you thought, or some unexpected expense blindsided you?

If I asked you right now what your total debt is and how much cash you have on hand, how long would it take for you to tell me?

How quickly could you show me what your monthly expenses are?

Like a clock, these numbers are ticking away 24 hours a day, seven days a week. They're not hard to access, either. So why should you ever be surprised by anything in your financial situation?

Obviously, I am excluding fraud or a partner or child racking up some costs without you knowing it. I have had at least a few friends who found out that their partners had been piling up credit-card debt behind their backs. Ouch!

If that ever happens to you, get a third party to help resolve it. You will be too frustrated and upset to solve it yourself and you will risk damaging your relationship in the process. Discovery is good, because now the truth is at hand and solutions can be sought with a banker or a counselor. Getting through a difficult time with someone you love can actually bring you closer and make the relationship stronger.

In a perverse way, navigating your way through a particularly difficult financial situation should make you a better money manager, but please don't use that notion as a reason to get there in the first place! "Hey, honey, I maxed out our credit cards as a learning exercise," probably won't achieve the desired end result.

Money issues, even small ones between friends, lovers and, yes, family members, can be extremely damaging if not well-handled. But that's for someone else's book. This book is just for and about you.

Managing money may seem like a daunting task, especially if you are behind in your understanding of the reality of your money.

At the most fundamental level, there are only four elements to your finances: 1) how much money you have coming in; 2) how much you need to spend for you and your dependents to survive with food, clothing and shelter; 3) how much you spend willingly each day on items that are not essential to survival; and 4) how much you are forced to repay because of debts you have incurred.

The most vital thing you can do to manage your finances is to get all of the facts in front of you, using those four categories as a starting point. Most of you will have many more cash output items than I have listed. You will likely need a "non-essential" category as well.

Remember: the truth will set you free.

If the information isn't readily at hand, don't look backward — look forward. Start gathering that information moment to moment, and day to day, for the next 60 days. You will then see where your cash comes from and, more importantly, where it goes.

The simple exercise of logging every cent that comes in and, crucially, every cent that goes out by amount, item, and by category as listed above, will create the awareness that is essential for you to improve your situation.

There is nothing fancy needed although, if it helps, you can download an income and expense tracker online or find a free online ledger that sets out columns and lines to help you bring order to your log.

Patterns will quickly start to emerge. I bet you will be surprised where money goes.

In my businesses, I regularly review all payments that go out. I can tell you that, even though we have a great team of finance people, I always find payments for things that we can do without or that may not have been properly reviewed.

The same will hold true in your personal life when you start to track exactly where every cent goes.

It is easy to add possessions or services to your expenses and forget to offload old ones that the new ones were intended to replace.

In my novel, *Critical Care*, I commented on consumerism through the voice of a character, Judge O'Reilly: "…we've plugged those roadside storage lockers with enough extra stuff to fill about half again as many homes as we have in this country…"

I must say, it is a bad sign of the state of our society when the storage-locker business is a high-growth industry.

When you begin your income and spending review, you will get a vivid snapshot of your life. You may have spent $25 at fast-food restaurants on multiple occasions; the visits to your local coffee shop cost more than you think; you dined out three times in the last two weeks; you were at the liquor store twice; you bought 48 bottles of bottled water; your mortgage payment is more than half your monthly income; you can just barely make the minimum payment on your credit card…

Welcome this discovery!

Facing your numbers can be a bit scary at first, but I bet you will start to get excited about these newfound insights and you will start to tell your friends. In turn, they will share that they are worried about their finances, too. You are now becoming a financial leader and it could well turn out that you and a couple of friends embark on this journey together.

You will likely see excess that you can trim without adversely affecting your lifestyle one iota. If you need more constraint to get back on track, so be it. You can do it. The single most important aspect of getting your financial house in order is having some professional help. That could be a bank, a retired volunteer with financial experience, a peer who is good with finances, an internet club or an investment group. Really, just the act of tracking and sharing the data with almost anyone will get you started. The road to financial ruin is pretty straightforward: Too much spending, not enough income.

Luckily, the road back to financial stability is equally straightforward. It just takes a bit of knowledge, a bit of discipline and a bit of time. Every baby step in the right direction is a good step on the journey to financial understanding and progress.

If you have been carrying an emotional burden based on financial anxiety, imagine how good it will feel to lay that burden down and lighten your load.

The best time to have started was yesterday, but the next-best time is today.

Your numbers are nothing more than an extension of you; be partners with them in a financially balanced life.

My father used to say, "When it comes to money, you have no friends."

I was young when I first heard that and it didn't mean much until I had some money and some friends. We all have friends who don't pay their share of the restaurant bill, or who are conveniently absent when the bar bill comes, or who borrow a fiver and forget to pay it back.

That stuff is annoying, but we can live with it.

I found out what my father meant when real money became involved.

People lend friends money to help them out, only to watch that friend continue to spend frivolously and delay paying back the loan.

People book expensive trips together and the friend that does the booking always seems to end up on the short side of the financial equation.

Families and friendships have been ruined in arguments over winning lottery tickets, inheritances and business deals that didn't work out.

So, how do we prevent that from happening?

The simple answer is to avoid financial transactions with friends and family who are not reliable or experienced in these matters. Just say, "No, I value you too much to let money ever get in between us."

If that answer ruins the relationship, just imagine how far south it would have gone if money had exchanged hands.

My experience has been that commerce, of any sort, with friends can strain those relationships; I've learned to keep friends and money at arm's-length from each other.

There are times, though, when we are able and want to help a friend or family member.

In that case, I have a few suggestions. 1) Give them a gift of money that is harmless to you and have no expectation of repayment. Tell them to "pay it forward" to someone else someday; 2) If the money is significant, involve a professional banker and offer a limited guarantee so that you are never the person causing the collection to happen. It is important to understand the risk you are taking and you must be able to afford to lose the money; 3) Always make a written agreement when monetary transactions are involved in amounts that have the potential to hurt either party. Just write up a simple agreement that outlines the terms and be sure to get an unrelated party to witness the signatures. Each party should also declare, in writing, that the other party has given them ample time to get external advice.

If the amount of money is significant, please involve a lawyer, and possibly an accountant, to assist you. Their fees will be well spent on the protection of your money and, perhaps more importantly, your relationship with the other party.

Getting these matters in writing, properly signed and witnessed, is important because sometimes things go wrong.

Most of us are optimists. We hope for the best and avoid thinking about the potential downsides of situations. I have been trained in business, through time and experience, to know that things can and do go wrong.

People die, are hurt in accidents, become ill, file for divorce, or just get lost in life and forget what they committed to. With your written document, at least you will have some evidence and leverage if you decide you want to try to collect the money.

You may have heard the saying that "health is the greatest wealth." I believe that to be true and yet, in an odd way, the poor management of money can create harm to your health from the constant stress of living beyond one's means.

The only thing I remember from the university economics course I dropped out of was that, in anticipation of higher income in the future or on the horizon, we develop a propensity to spend. Often, though, the higher income fails to materialize and the pre-spending has already been done. This could be buying a bigger house, a better car, a cottage, booking a big trip, loading up on new furniture, or even deciding to have more children or get a dog. All these commitments will require more cash down the road.

Then, there you find yourself, stalled in your career, or worse. Please avoid this trap.

It is vital to understand that money is not real until it is in your bank account. Financial gains on real estate, the stock market or other investments are just on paper. Equity and assets are not real until they have been liquidated and you have the cash (and have put aside a reserve for taxes).

In finance, in particular, anything that sounds too good to be true probably is too good to be true. There's no such thing as "get rich quick." Few of us win lotteries. Nothing you invest in is fail-safe, including real estate.

Sorry, but that's the hard truth. Even millionaires get duped in Ponzi schemes, and they like to think they're pretty sophisticated investors. You and I really have to exercise caution.

So remember, like it or not, you and your numbers do have a meeting coming up. Your numbers are always ready for the meeting; it's time for you to be, too.

TEN

TIME — never will time away.

How often have you said something like, "Oh, I can't wait for this week to be over…," or "this day to end," or "next summer," or "winter to end"?

Time's up.

Time-out.

Time flies.

Time will tell.

What time is it?

Where does time go?

I can be a little obsessed by time, because it is so precious.

When I warm up something in the microwave and watch 120 seconds tick by, I lament that time passing, never to be relived or regained.

I long for the Holodeck from Star Trek so I can relive time!

Alas, I don't count on that technology arriving any time soon, so I try to make the best of every moment of every day.

Essentially, that is what this book is about: sharing some of my thoughts and experiences that may help you get more out of the time you have.

No doubt you have heard the saying that life can change in an instant or a second. It's true — a chance glance at the partner of your dreams…a car accident narrowly avoided…a bird gleaming spectacularly in just the right light…a peek up at the night sky just as a meteor, satellite or space station sails overhead…a bus just caught or missed…

We awake each day with 86,400 seconds to spend in the next 24 hours.

That's a lot of seconds!

How would you like to spend them?

The great thing is that, for most, they renew each morning for many years. For some, the years are cut short — in a second. Others may become a hero — in a second. Some might break a heart — in a second. Or take a life — in a second. Or make a life — in a second. Or, or, or…

We often hear how time seems to speed up as we get older, or how summer used to last forever when we were young.

One year to a five-year-old is fully 20 percent of his life passing, whereas one year to a forty-year-old is a mere 2.5 percent of his life passing. For an eighty-year-old, though, it is just a blink of an eye. Math might explain why time seems to accelerate as we age.

"Time flies when you're having fun," they say, and I agree.

Ever notice how fast that one- or two-week holiday zips by?

Ever notice how the same length of time working on a project that is a "must do," as opposed to a "want to do," can seem to drag on?

I find that fascinating and, with that knowledge, I try to make the best of every moment.

I was once told about the dirtiest jobs we inevitably all face or have to do in life that, "If you can't get out of it, get into it!"

In other words, find the joy in the struggle somehow because you have no option but to do it. It can seem that much of life is toil with intermittent periods of joy. We could equate that to the climbers of Everest who risk their lives toiling mightily for days for a few minutes of jubilation at the summit.

My father used to give me "dirty jobs" like mowing acres of grass, picking weeds in the raspberry patch, or grooming the field free of stones — by hand!

"Go cut grass," he'd say, "and think about your future."

If you have trouble finding the pleasure or joy in whatever you're toiling away at, that task may pass slowly and possibly feel like drudgery.

Somehow I figured out how to feel rewarded after a dirty job: do it well and with a good attitude.

I hear people doing what I call, "Willing time away."

"I can't wait until Friday."

"I can't wait until this job is done."

"I can't wait to get there."

This is living in anticipation of something better to come.

"If I had a better job, I would be more productive."

"If I had a bigger house, I would be happier."

"If I had more money, less debt, a better boss, a new partner, nicer clothes, better neighbors, thinner legs, more hair, a new lawnmower and time to cut the grass, I would be happier."

But what about right now?

What if time doesn't deliver what you long for? What if you haven't actually got as much time as you think?

Joy or drudgery? Which do you choose?

People ask me how I get so much done or how I have been able to accumulate so many life experiences.

I am always flattered by the question and, to be honest, I don't really think about it very often.

However, the answer I have become most comfortable with is, "I cherish time and try to use it wisely."

I appreciate and have become quite deliberate in my use of the gift of time. That is not to say that I never waste any. It's just that when I do flop on the couch for an hour, or indulge in a cheesy television show, I am wasting time consciously and happily. I enjoy it without guilt.

It would be totally counterproductive to beat myself up for a little bit of layabout behavior.

Procrastination, though, is another thing all together. Are you a procrastinator? Do you want to get back to me on that?

I wasn't always a productive guy. I did not find the joy in university so I procrastinated with the might of a warrior and dragged along anyone who would follow.

All night ping-pong, seemingly never-ending games of Risk, early morning trips to the vending machines for flaky pastry fruit tarts warmed up in the microwave and washed down with cold milk and, yes, lots and lots of partying.

In the summer, after my miserable first year, I received a letter from the Dean of our school. Yes me, a letter from the Dean. It informed that I had made his list — for academic probation. Unfortunately for me, and much to the ire of my financial backer (my father), it was not the Dean's list I had been sent there to make.

I was given exactly one more semester to get my grades up or I would be "asked" to leave the school.

After that dismal first year, I dropped out of economics and psychology. I somehow found my way into some great law and criminology courses that really captured my mind.

In first year, I had missed a lot of classes and I was lousy at studying. Textbooks were my cure for insomnia.

In second year, though, I made a point of going to all my classes and taking notes. I didn't study much harder, but when I reviewed my notes, I realized that I actually knew the material.

I started to manage my time better and now, looking back, I realize I was becoming more deliberate in my actions. At the time, I didn't realize what was improving. For me, it was all about survival. Necessity is the mother of invention, as they say.

If only for competitive reasons, I was determined to be the first in my family to earn a university degree.

In early December, I was called to the office of my second-year Law 200 professor. I was sure that I was in deep trouble. I sat down and looked across the desk at him. He had been my Law 100 professor as well and, because I was living on campus, he knew more about me than he did about off-campus students.

"How do you think you did on the mid-term?"

I took a deep breath. "I have no idea."

"No idea?"

"Nope."

"Well, whatever you are doing this year, just keep it up."

"Sir, I have worked a lot harder this year and am trying to do better."

"No, no, I wasn't being sarcastic. You got the highest mark out of 300 students. Keep up the good work. I knew you could do this if you just applied yourself. You have it inside, just let it out."

I was 18 years old and that professor was the first person in my adult life to give me sincere encouragement and support. It was the positive reinforcement of people like him that slowly nudged me onto the right path with a few encouraging words.

I was elated. I had a taste of how the proper allocation of my time could be rewarded and I wanted more. In hindsight, I also was learning how to learn. It turns out that I am an auditory visual learner. If I hear it when I see it, I get it. Reading alone never was, and still never is, the best way for me to learn. In the meanwhile, time had become my friend and I began using it diligently. I became productive.

I just kept improving academically. I had many other mountains to climb, but I had the school thing in hand. I did graduate. I even wrote the LSAT, but I'm glad now I wasn't accepted into a law school.

Okay, so when you wake up tomorrow, you will be gifted 86,400 seconds to spend in the 24 hours that follow.

I encourage you to use each one as though it is the most precious resource you have. Time is freely given, yet can so easily be taken away.

Unwrap that gift carefully.

ELEVEN

POSITIVE — are you building or diminishing with your words?

How often have you witnessed the impact that a positive approach can have on a difficult situation?

Why do you think we can be so attracted to the negative aspects of life?

A while back, our hometown newspaper ran a wonderful front-page story about a very long journey a love letter had taken to find its intended recipient. A soldier had mailed it to his sweetheart and, after many years, it had finally found its way to her. The story was funny, warm and touched my heart.

I bumped into the then-publisher of the paper at a charity event shortly thereafter and expressed my appreciation for the story.

"It's great to see some good news on the front page," I told him. "I hope it sold well for you."

"Unfortunately, no," he replied. "It sold very poorly. Today, bad news sells papers," he lamented.

Why do we gravitate to the misery of others rather than celebrate their joy?

How has humor become such that the joke is always on someone else? I call it "take-away" humor: humor that detracts from someone else to get the laugh.

By the time I took my life-changing trip to Africa, I was finished with derogatory humor and wanted something new to get laughs from.

Very early in life, I developed what I guess was some sort of protective mechanism — a very sharp tongue. The first thought and, subsequently, the first words were typically a sharp remark at someone to deflect negative attention from me onto them.

I am not sure how it started, but I became a master of the put-down.

Luckily for me, when the light in my soul got switched on in Africa, all that changed. I was able to rewire myself to look for the good or opportunity in every situation instead of the negative.

Of course, I am still often challenged by negative initial thoughts. I have just learned how to "let the first thought go" and give my heart a chance to speak. I am not foolproof. In times of weakness, I can still say stupid or hurtful things. Now, though, the second I do say something negative, I recognize it and quickly rephrase, apologize or follow up with something that neutralizes my misspeak.

Here's an example that I often use to explain take-away humor. It used to be that when I bumped into someone I knew, in a place where I didn't expect to see them, I would say, "You see the craziest people in the nicest places!" Everyone would chuckle, of course, and maybe the person would feel a bit sheepish or put down, but I didn't care because I got the laugh.

Today I say, "Hey, you meet the nicest people in the craziest places!" Guess what? I still get the laugh, but this time the person feels good about the compliment.

Subtle difference — big impact. Such is life. It truly is the little things that matter.

We are constantly surrounded by negativity in the news, on TV, in magazines, in other people. In many cases, courtesy has been replaced by aggression. Have you tried to cross a street as a pedestrian lately?

The good news is that it is so easy now to stand out in the crowd, to be a beacon of positive light in our dark world, so to speak.

How many couples do you know that pick on each other constantly? Who would choke on their words before they would compliment their partner in front of friends?

I once confronted two friends of mine on that very issue. The three of us had been the best of buddies and I was regularly at their home for dinner. The negative comments flying between them got to the point of making me uncomfortable. They were struggling in their relationship, for sure.

I finally said, "You know, I haven't heard you ever say one positive thing to each other in the many years I have been coming here."

Many people just don't hear themselves and I thought that maybe my friends were just numb or oblivious to their own words.

To the contrary, and to my surprise, they both acknowledged their behavior as "just the way it is" between them.

They divorced shortly thereafter.

When couples do that to each other, especially in front of others, I call it "death by a thousand comments."

Now, imagine this: imagine how it would be if everything you say to every person in your life, from this day forward, was positive and made them feel better.

A man named Lou Tice, of The Pacific Institute, offered up a great verb: "be-Big."

"Rather than be-little people," he said to us, "be-Big them!"

The choice is yours. It's your thoughts, your attitude, your voice, your words.

I work hard, in personal and professional relationships, to express gratitude, pride and love in my conversations.

I can feel you getting squeamish.

It takes a bit of work at first if this is something that you are not used to doing, but the rewards are instant and immeasurable.

Somewhere along the line, parents sometimes stop telling their kids that they love them and vice versa.

It is always interesting when I speak to groups and ask the men in the crowd, "How many of you have told your fathers that you love them?"

Suffice it to say, not a lot of hands, if any, go up.

On my dad's seventieth birthday, I decided to give him a gift of positivity.

He had not had the easiest life and that experience had shaped him into someone who didn't express positive emotions easily.

We were gathered at the kitchen table for his birthday dinner at our family home. Prior to the cake coming out, I told him that I had a gift for him. I asked him to walk upstairs to the family room to accept it.

"No, no," he declined. "Go get it and bring it down here."

"I can't. You have to come upstairs."

As I write this for you, this memory is crystal clear and not without emotion on my part.

I got quite upset and began to insist that he bend to my will. "You have to come up," I repeated more than once.

His resolve only hardened.

Finally, the frustration was too much for me to bear. I am not proud of what I said next. "Fine. Listen. I have a fucking present for you and it is fucking upstairs. Now get up and come with me or forget it and I will leave now."

Shazam. He sprung to his feet and, without saying a word, followed me upstairs. Needless to say, the dining room behind us was silent.

When we arrived in the family room on the second floor, I closed the door and asked him to sit down. He complied. It seemed that the walk up the stairs had calmed us both.

"I wanted to give you a special gift for your seventieth birthday," I started.

My words did not come easily.

"I got thinking that I can't remember the last time I told you I loved you or that you told me that you loved me."

I started to cry and choked on the next words.

"So my gift to you today is to tell you that I love you very much and to thank you for being a good father to me."

Dad was now crying quietly as he watched me speak.

"Of course I love you," he said.

"Maybe so, but you have never told me."

Tears poured down his cheeks as he stood up and put his arms around me. I could feel his slim body shake with sobs.

At my age now, I feel that I can only imagine what must have been going through his mind. That was the first of only a few times in my adult life when I had an intimate verbal and emotional experience with my father. I am really very glad that it happened and I hope that this inspires you to do the same with one or both of your parents.

Not long after that, my dad's health began to wane and a short ten years later he was gone.

For that decade, as difficult as it was, I worked hard to keep "emotionally current" with him. When he died at eighty, I had no regrets about not having shared my positive feelings with him. It was so much more liberating and healthier than dwelling on some of the negativity that family life can generate.

When you think about your life, or even one moment, one day, or one relationship in it, what do you ultimately want out of it?

Do you want the negative, the neutral or the positive?

Are you concerned that your negative friends might not like you anymore if you change and only see and say the positive in life?

Be a leader. Set an example. You will be surprised at how easy and how powerful seeing the roses, rather than the thorns, can be.

TWELVE

MOMENTUM — you can't coast out of a pothole.

How often have you felt that you are in a rut and just can't get going?

You're busy, right? Never enough time to get done what needs to be done, let alone what you want to get done?

No time for sleep, let alone holidays?

Do you find that, even in rare down-time, you are busy worrying about all the things that could go wrong? Can the "what-if" mode consume you?

Then, out of the blue, it happens. You hit the wall. Suddenly, you genuinely don't know what to do next. It feels like you are in a state of suspended animation. The phone isn't ringing, people aren't bothering you, no one is home or maybe no deadline looms, yet you still feel like you just can't get going.

You look at the tasks in front of you. You scan some to-do lists only to see that the tasks are done or not appropriate for that moment. You almost feel a little panic coming on because you are a get-things-done person, right?

You are like a shiny, fast, well-tuned car stuck in a rut; the engine is running, but you just can't get going.

What do you do?

As I write, I realize that this happens to me often, and has been happening throughout my career. Writers call it writer's block. Maybe for you we can call it "doer's block."

I am lucky because, as a business owner, I can, for the most part, create my own schedule. I lead a strong team so I don't need to be present though I am always "on the clock," so to speak.

I discovered this unusual phenomenon I call "doer's block" early in my career. I uncovered a very simple concept that I call "finish a task — any task — and build on small accomplishments."

The whole idea was to get some momentum going when I got stuck in a rut.

This situation and these symptoms could be at work, on your diet, in some fight against a challenge, during your athletic training or even in your relationships. It does happen and it doesn't matter why.

We are fueled by momentum. We need progress in every aspect of our lives.

Even in writing this, I need to build momentum. I don't always feel like writing, but I always feel good after I do and that is what keeps me going: focusing on the end result.

When I am challenged to find the motivation to write, I pick an easy topic to cover so the words and thoughts flow. I often write twice as much as I thought I would.

Action is your friend, your brain isn't. The brain, supposedly the source of our intellect, seems to be the laziest muscle we have. My brain will always urge me to do something that is less, rather than more, challenging.

I rarely want to work out, for instance, even though I have been a competitive athlete most of my life.

I do love the result, though, so I overpower the brain that would have me sleep in or turn on the TV. I don the running shoes or grab my bathing suit, goggles and towel and get my butt out the door.

I focus on the end result as opposed to the obstacles my brain is transmitting.

I am not sure what part of my brain I tap into, but I heard a good concept from Lou Tice of The Pacific Institute called "flash back — flick forward."

It means that when faced with a challenge, flash back to a similar challenge and focus on how you got over it and what the positive end result was. Then flick that vision forward to the present and get your butt in gear!

Whether the task at hand is exercise, diet, work, a relationship issue, an addiction issue or anything else, when you have lost momentum, simply break it down into smaller parts.

By tackling something small, you will likely finish it quickly, and well, and gain a small sense of accomplishment.

One small step for you, so to speak, and one giant step toward building new momentum.

In your work environment, you might take 15 minutes to clean off a shelf that has been getting loaded with junk. "Wow! It's done, it's clean, it looks good, I did it!"

Maybe you will tidy a file, a drawer or your desk, or clean your computer keyboard, similarly small but rewarding tasks.

A few things happen when you do this. First, it distracts you from whatever is blocking your other progress. Second, it actually achieves something that needed to be done but never got prioritized. Third, you will get a little endorphin boost from the sense of accomplishment. Watch the magic happen as your clarity returns and the work that you were stuck on now seems glaringly obvious or doable. Off you go once again!

Be careful, though, to avoid a prolonged cleaning frenzy. If you don't get the boost you seek in fairly short order, you may want to just get out of the building. Take a walk, or cut and run, if possible, but do something completely different.

If you fell off your diet, don't try to recapture the progress all in one day. Just nudge yourself gently back in the right direction.

If you messed up a relationship, tackle one aspect of the problem or transgression first and build back your credibility slowly, gently and lovingly. It takes time to heal the heart.

If you are kicking an addiction, reduce, reduce, reduce and know that setbacks happen and are to be expected. The main thing is you are making progress toward your goal.

If you neglected your workouts, just head out for a brisk walk, ride or run, no matter how brief. Hey, just put on your workout clothes. I find that kicks me into gear.

A former competitive running friend of mine said something that has stayed with me for decades and still motivates me through the ups and downs of keeping fit.

He said, "Phillip, it is better to run a half a mile a day every day for ten days, than to go out and run five miles every tenth day."

Simple, yet powerful.

Just getting out the door, so to speak, and getting on with nibbling the small bites in life makes taking the big bites so much easier.

Professional sports announcers, and even the athletes themselves, talk about momentum and "getting back to the basics" as a way of boosting their game.

There is a great diagram that may help you figure out what is holding you back and killing momentum. It has four quadrants showing how to prioritize so we focus in on what most needs our attention. It's divided into urgent and important; not urgent but important; urgent but not important; not urgent and not important. Easily found online, it helps you determine high and low priorities, their impacts, and what action you need (or don't need) to take. What to worry about and what to let go of.

Mark Twain is quoted as saying, "I've had a lot of worries in my life, most of which never happened."

It is easy to get caught up in the "what if" and lose momentum by being distracted from focusing on the now. It is kind of like thinking about the sky, then the stars, then the Milky Way, then the universe. Suddenly, it is overwhelming and you can't move, right?

Try to get on with what is most likely to happen, and allow yourself only to think about the "might" or "could" as a way to be generally aware of the world around you.

I suggest that you avoid putting any time into "not likely to happen," even though it is easy to get caught up in speculative swirl and kill that forward motion you are seeking.

My experience, so far, is that most of life pretty well works out as it should, when it should. It only gets uncomfortable when we try to manipulate or rush the natural course of things.

Focusing on the here and now will help you keep your personal momentum going.

When we have momentum, we feel better. We act better. We give off and subsequently get better vibes bouncing back. That makes us happy, which helps us keep our momentum going, and the whole process just keeps repeating.

I know it sounds like I'm oversimplifying things, but hear me out.

Have you ever pushed a car out of a snowdrift or a muddy rut? Have you ever had to move a big object across a beach or a lawn?

You likely remember that the best way to do that is to gently rock the car or object back and forth in rhythm with the other people who may be helping you.

Small, gentle moves, back and forth. Back and forth. Back and forth and forward you go with the momentum you have created.

So if tomorrow you find yourself in one of life's many potholes, just stop.

Take a breath.

Set the task aside altogether.

Do something else for a while. Choose something small that you know can be accomplished with ease, yet will be worthwhile.

Watching TV or eating junk food, out of frustration, doesn't count.

Go ahead, you can do it. Finish a task, any task, and get your momentum going again!

THIRTEEN

SILENCE — is golden.

How do you feel about silence?

How often are you even exposed to it in a 24-hour period?

Do you wake to the radio?

Do you fall asleep with the television on?

Do you wear earphones and listen to music when you go for a walk, run or ride in nature?

How comfortable are you driving in a car with someone when no one is talking and there is no music playing?

When you do end up in silence, what is going on in your head?

Do you like what you hear?

Or are you afraid to listen?

When is the last time you tuned into the noise in your brain? The noise only you can hear?

I have been very fortunate to have traveled to some pretty cool places: Mount Kilimanjaro, the Serengeti and the Ruwenzori Mountains in Africa, the Daintree Rain Forest and Great Barrier Reef in Australia, the Andes Mountains in Venezuela, numerous other wonderful countries and, of course, coast to coast in Canada.

While I love the sights and sounds of big cities, I really appreciate the silence of nature — places devoid of manmade noise or objects.

High up one of the Andes Mountains of Venezuela, I paused and looked around. I could see no human imprint. Not one pole or tower, building or vehicle. There was just me, my horse and a few fellow journeyers.

I went off on my own for a bit, dismounted, and just stood there and listened.

My horse's breathing was the only sound I could hear. I realized that I was standing on soil that had never been tilled or turned by man. This pristine spot had been this way since time immemorial.

I can't recall specifically what thoughts or conversations were going on in my head. My overriding memory is total peace, feeling privileged to be having that experience.

As a scuba diver, one of the things I enjoy most, over and above the visuals, is the lack of sound beyond the inhalations and exhalations of my breath.

As a pilot, I love the great vistas from high up in the air. There is some background noise from the plane, but it can be a relatively silent experience if I am flying alone.

As I write for you, it is just me and my keyboard. No other sounds — just the clicking of the keys, for hours and hours, with the occasional lonely call of a foghorn on the ferry that crosses near where I live. Today it's a thick, foggy morning; it seems to blanket and muffle a lot of the ambient noise.

So, how do you feel about silence?

One of the challenges of going from constant noise to silence is what I call the "wind-down."

Have you ever been in a museum or church, where silence is requested or expected? Were you able to stay quiet while appreciating those revered places, or were you one of the people who got disapproving glances from others or had to be shushed? Did that annoy you or make you aware?

Have you ever tried to listen to a speech, but the people at the back of the room just can't keep quiet?

Both of these scenarios drive me nuts. I am actually the guy who will ask people to keep quiet. No, it's not always popular, but it's usually effective because often people just aren't aware of the noises they're making.

They are victims of the "wind-down": it's like a motor or fan that spins for a while, even after the power is turned off.

The brain can be the same. It's constantly spinning, whirring and working away for you, and hard to instantly turn off.

When you power down external noise, internal noise may actually seem louder for a while, now that it is unmasked. Perhaps that is why it is so hard to suddenly become quiet. Many are tempted to power back up the external noise because they can't take internal noise. The switch from audio and visual to just visual can be hard to flick.

Give silence some time.

Be patient with your brain while it adjusts.

Have you ever seen a film about bats leaving a cave at dusk?

Think of the cave as your mind and the bats as the cacophony of deafening noise that rattles around inside your head.

In time, the noise dies down; the bats eventually vacate the cave.

As we go through each day, jamming our heads full of useless noise, we need to remember that our heads need time to adjust.

Have you ever been home sick in bed and actually had no desire to hear any noise?

Have you noticed, after a day or two, that you start to think about things that you hadn't thought of in years? Old friends, old stories, old memories come drifting back into your consciousness.

That is the beauty of silence.

I spent seven months in Africa in my mid-thirties. When I arrived, my heart, mind and soul were so jammed up with life that there was no room for anything else.

All I seemed to do for the first few weeks was sleep and cry. While that isn't exactly true, it does give you an idea of how burnt-out I was when I arrived. I now realize that I slept to nourish my body and I cried to empty my mind and soul. I wasn't sad; I was full.

I am sure you have read about our bodies being vessels for our souls. Our lives are essentially reactions to the stuff we put in that vessel.

Put junk in every day and voila: a junky life. Put good in every day and I believe life is far more joyous and rewarding.

If we decide to change our path and add new stuff to our vessel, it's just like it is with a closet full of old clothes. We need to make new room by discarding some other things.

What I know now, that I didn't know back in Africa, was that my body and brain were just automatically cleansing themselves. They were getting ready for something new, something better. Silence and time with nature, deep in Uganda, was my healing place.

One sunny African morning, I walked out onto the roof of one of the buildings that connected to the children's school where I was staying. I was on a backpacker's budget so this place was ideal. Despite it being the Christmas season, the hills were a verdant green. The schoolchildren were on holidays, but I could faintly hear other locals making their daily pilgrimage along the road, containers in hand, to the only water source in that area. They pretty much walked in silence or sang soft songs.

I felt different. The sun seemed warmer. The greens seemed greener. The air was alive as it entered and exited my body.

I had been in Uganda for three or four weeks. No booze. No processed foods. No television or other electronics. Lots of vegetables. Lots of sleeping and crying.

I was rested. Silence had been my helper and my healer.

The good news is you don't have to go far at all to find silence and nature. Not at all.

Most of our world is filled with it.

Give silence a chance. Be open to, and aware of, the various stages your mind goes through as you withdraw from noise. You never know — you just may discover a hidden or forgotten talent.

Ideas or inspirations will appear from seemingly nowhere when, in reality, they have just been hidden in the fog of a busy life.

What's the worst that can happen?

The world's manmade noise will always be there if you find that you miss it. I predict, though, that you will just enjoy some silence and, in the end, it will become a faithful companion in your life journey.

If you are used to the noise, though, and are not sure how to get started, take a quiet walk, alone, in the woods.

Sit on your deck or in your yard.

Take a bike ride, or a ride in your car with the radio off.

Remove the television or computer from your bedroom. You can always put them back.

Try to end your day ideally: in love and in silence.

If you don't wake up easily and need an alarm of some sort, try waking to the sounds of wind, ocean waves or birds that alarms now offer. You can always set a second wake-up with a blaring siren in case the first one fails you.

I hope that once you tune into silence, you will hear things that you have not heard for a long time or perhaps have never heard.

Mostly you will hear yourself, and that is a beautiful thing to listen to.

FOURTEEN

SORRY — one of the most powerful words in personal and professional growth.

How often have you struggled within and resisted saying "I am sorry" to someone, only to be surprised at the wonderful response you got and the immense relief you felt having uttered the words?

Right now, I bet you can think of one or more people to whom a good, old-fashioned apology would go a long way.

"I am sorry" have to be the three most powerful words we can harness for growth.

I don't mean an empty, perfunctory or hollow "I am sorry." I mean a thoughtful, sincere and heartfelt expression of regret, delivered so the receiving party truly feels your emotion.

A solid "I am sorry" should elicit a hug, handshake, warm smile, sometimes tears or, other times, intimacy. Personal intimacy. Intimacy with your partner. It will almost always initiate a dialogue that immediately builds up the relationship.

Timing is, of course, important and doing it in person, if possible, is the best way to offer up an apology.

If the words can't be exchanged in person, over the telephone is the next best alternative. People should hear your remorse. Barring that, a hand-written, snail-mailed note should capture your remorse. In my opinion, defaulting to email, text or your favorite social media channel will diminish the impact.

Picking the perfect time and place can be a challenge, so give it some thought. Sometimes the words need to be spoken in front of peers to right a commonly known wrong.

"Listen, while we are all together, I want to say to Bob here that I am really sorry for that comment I made the other night. It was not well thought-out and didn't come out the way I wanted it to. I hope you guys can forgive me."

In the workplace, things move fast and egos bruise easily. I bet that I say "I am sorry" to a co-worker at least once a month.

I go to their office, ask for a minute and get right to the point.

"Hey, about that meeting, I am sorry that I cut you off mid-sentence. That wasn't appropriate. I value you and our relationship and want to let you know that."

If you are in a leadership role, making sincere use of the words "I am sorry" can be an important tool to forge loyalty and cooperative spirit amongst your team. Not only is it the smart thing to do, it is the right thing to do.

Lead by example. Humility is a powerful quality in a leader.

With loved ones, don't wait and let the hurt fester. You know when you are out of line because your wise inner bird tells you right away. Just double back and fix it ASAP with your lover, your kids, your spouse or your neighbor.

Life is bumpy and we all say and do things that we regret.

If you imagine life's road as one that eventually doubles back on itself — one that you will travel over and over again, thinking "I've been here, done this before" — imagine each hurtful thing you say or do as a rock that you drop on that road.

Life's road usually starts out smoothly. It is the pebbles, stones and boulders that we drop along the way that we run over in the future. Then we wonder why life has gotten bumpy all of a sudden.

Saying "I am sorry" can also be a healing catalyst for someone who has offended you who just doesn't know how to start the dialogue.

Be the big person and create the opportunity for them to grow.

Let's say that someone offends or embarrasses you, alone or in front of others, in a work or social setting. You let it go, but you haven't forgotten, and now there is tension in the relationship. You know that the other person should apologize to you but hasn't, can't or won't.

In a sincere way, try to help them.

"You know that other day when you said (what was said)? That surprised me and hurt my feelings. I wonder if maybe I have done or said something that offended you, or if I just misinterpreted what you meant? I just want to say that I am really sorry if that is the case."

You have opened up an opportunity for healing. Your friend or colleague now has the chance to share what is on their mind. It may not always work, but there is no downside to trying.

The fact is that people are mostly good, but sometimes behave badly. Behavioral systems are often signaling a deeper rooted issue within that person. This underlying "dis-ease" can sometimes prompt us into awkward situations or cause dumb things to be said with no ability to fix them.

If you come at this from a heartfelt place, you can not only improve your personal situation, but also build deep bonds of trust with others.

Upon my return from Africa, I made a list of people I felt I needed to apologize to.

My "I am sorry" list went all the way back to high school and crossed many divides in my personal and professional life. Over a period of a few years, I reached out to about ten people and expressed regret for something I had done or said to them that I knew had been hurtful. The most interesting thing to me was how gracious every single person was. Most had completely forgotten the situation or words, because time has a way of healing wounds.

Reaching out to others lifted a load off my heart that I hadn't realized I was carrying. It was a potent experience, the greatest of which happened on Canada's Prince Edward Island. I had been a water-ski coach there when I was 18.

I look back at myself then and see just how little I knew and how lost I was. I was getting by on raw street knowledge, decent looks, a nice smile and a fast tongue. Luckily, I also had a pretty good set of technical skills that had some value and was a fairly talented water skier.

The man I worked for that summer loved to swear, wisecrack, flirt and generally keep people on their toes with his sharp tongue. Funnily enough, he was married to a most delightful woman. They had no kids, but each summer took a new coach to their oceanfront cabin to train the locals to water-ski. That year, I was the new coach. I lived with them, like a son, in their home.

I soon learned that swearing in front of "mother" was verboten, so my boss and I took to using the word "frig."

"Friggin' this and friggin' that." He laughed and seemed to love it and we frigged our friggin' way through the entire friggin' summer, ticking mother off with every utterance of the word. It seemed that he enjoyed teasing his wife and now he had a ready accomplice.

I teased "mother" about her meditation.

I put ketchup on her delicious dinners.

I stayed out way too late and worried her.

Together, he and I teased and cajoled her all summer long. On the final day of my job, she blew her top at me. She told me how ungrateful I was, what a brat I was, that I had ruined her summer, brought sin and evil into her house, sullied her cooking, and disrespected her God.

Yikes…this woman actually had something to say and, believe me, I was listening.

Beneath all my bravado was a motherless boy just trying to make some friends and have some fun. I guess I knew inside that what I was doing was hurtful. It just didn't fully register at the time. I was one shocked kid as I pulled out of their driveway to catch the ferry, head to Ottawa, and check into my university dorm room.

It was too late for apologies. I would never be asked back and she had warned me never to ask for a reference, because it wouldn't be a good one.

I drove non-stop through the night from PEI directly to Carleton University. Even today, I can remember how bright that night was with a huge moon to light the way. I recall turning off my headlights for a long period of time and driving by moonlight, just to show I could, I guess.

As the person I was back then, I accepted that the harm was done. Nothing I could do about it. "Whatever," or "screw them," I likely thought to myself. "He shouldn't have encouraged me and she got what she deserved!" Yep, sad to say that's about what I would have thought back then.

Some twenty-one years later, I was back on Prince Edward Island, a different Phillip with a basket of new life tools that were helping me shape a new, post-Africa me.

This was another big "I am sorry" that I wanted to say. I had never been back in contact with that man or woman. I had no idea if they still lived in the same house or even if they were alive. I drove slowly from Charlottetown, wondering what I would find. The long, dusty driveway hadn't changed. I could still see the North River, off in the distance, where I had spent the better part of every day driving a water-ski boat that summer, and teaching kids the sport.

My heart sank. My mouth dried. There was the house. It looked exactly the same as I remembered it. There was a car there, but no sign of people. I wondered if they still lived there and if they were home.

I knocked on the screen door.

It opened and I locked eyes with the man who had been my partner in crime (or so I had thought) so many years ago.

He looked the same.

Everything seemed to move into slow motion. Without expression, he tried to slam the door in my face.

Sometimes in life the most important decisions are made in an instant and governed only by instinct.

I jammed my food in the doorway and stopped the door dead in its swing.

He pushed once, and then paused.

I will never know what went through his mind. He could have grabbed a gun, shot me and claimed self-defense.

"Hey, it's me, Phillip Brown, from way back in the '70s."

"I know who you are," he muttered.

"I was in the area and I hoped that 'mother' might be home. I wanted to say hello to her."

"She's not here," he said from behind the door.

"Oh, okay." I knew from my experience that she never left the island without him. "I'm here for a few days," I lied. "When do you expect her back?"

"I don't know."

"Who is it, dear?"

It was her voice.

Silence.

"Oh, I guess she's back. I didn't hear her come in."

The door swung slowly open and there she was.

I am sure she had aged, but she looked exactly the same to me.

"Hello," she greeted me.

The three of us stood in momentary silence, as though no time had passed. The feelings seemed as raw as they were the day I drove out of that laneway so many summers before.

"Hello. Listen, I am very sorry to surprise you like this. It's been a long time since I saw you. I just have a few things I need to tell you and then I will leave."

My old boss receded into the distance, but there was nowhere in that small house where anyone's words were private.

She beckoned me back into the house that she had so firmly ejected me from many years earlier and waited.

"I came here today," I finally managed, " to tell you how very sorry I am that I treated you so badly the summer I stayed here." My eyes blurred. Tears ran down my face. My throat tightened. "I just didn't know better then and now I do. I also want to tell you that I understand and respect your faith and your meditation. Do you still meditate?"

She nodded.

"Well, I understand now. You were so good to me that summer and I do truly appreciate that. I just didn't know it at the time. I know you said you cared for me and that you prayed for me and I didn't get that, either. But now I do."

She smiled through moist eyes.

"I guess I just want to say I am sorry and let you know that, despite what you saw back then, I turned out okay and I get it now."

We hugged. We cried. She held me like her son and gazed into my eyes.

"Thank you," she said. "Thank you."

He didn't appear again, but I knew he had heard my words.

I drove slowly back up the red, dusty road with a lighter heart and another incredible life lesson learned.

"I am sorry" may be the hardest words to say. But their power will liberate you and lift others up.

Go ahead. Give them a try and witness this miracle yourself.

FIFTEEN

AUTHENTICITY — finding the real you.

Have you ever thought you knew someone really well and then, one day, discovered you didn't know them at all?

Who is the most real or authentic person you know and how do you feel about him or her?

What is it that attracts us to people who we view as being real or authentic?

I was mulling this over when a friend delivered a healthy baby last week, her third daughter.

She and I do not live in the same city but, through the magic of technology, family members, friends from around the world and I have had numerous opportunities to see the new baby. It's as though she were right in the same room.

When we look at this precious gem, we see her for exactly what she is: a helpless little person who needs assistance with everything. She doesn't try to be, or pretend to be, anything but what she is. The entire world sees her truth. She is, figuratively, and most of the time literally, naked to us.

This is the way we all begin our lives and interaction with the world around us.

It is often the way we leave our lives, too.

Another friend of mine recently had a severe stroke and died a few days later. Luckily, she did not suffer. Her end of life was sad, but it was also mercifully swift.

As is often the case, people said things like, "Well, if I have to go, I hope it's as quick," or, "At least she didn't suffer."

As with the newborn baby, we see those who are about to leave us as exactly who and what they are: helpless people who need assistance with everything. They don't try to be, nor for that matter can they pretend to be, anything but what they are. The entire world sees their truth. They, too, are figuratively naked to us.

For most people, including me, the journey from birth on isn't as simple as one might hope. Somehow we tend to create a divide — a tension if you will — between who we truly are and what we want the world to believe we are.

Imagine an elastic between your two thumbs. One thumb is the real you and one thumb is the you that you want the world to see.

When these two ends pull apart, we start to live with a tension between the two points of view.

This could be as simple as behaving strongly when we are weak, behaving bravely when we are scared, or behaving badly toward others when inside we are gentle.

It could be more complex — spending beyond one's means to create an impression of success, hiding an addiction, or cheating on a partner while pretending to be faithful.

Self-deception or false depiction can be complex. It can get to the point of disease. One lives a dual life with the second life being one of crime, perversion or violence, while maintaining a public facade of civility or even honor.

The rub is that, in the end, we always end up back at a point where, like the baby or the dying person, the world sees us naked and as we truly are.

Bad behavior can lead friends to ostracize you and get in the way of a personal goal. Debt catches up and severe cutbacks or bankruptcy may ensue. Hidden addiction takes a huge toll and can cost the ultimate price. Philandering breaks up families. Criminal or perverted behavior is revealed. Eventually, like the Wizard of Oz, the world will see the truth behind the curtain.

Bad or sad childhoods are often blamed.

I was lucky. For a while.

My infancy and youngest years were, by most standards, charmed — healthy, safe, well-fed and well-loved.

But when I was six, my world began to crumble. I watched and listened as my rock, my mother, suffered over a period of five years and ultimately succumbed to cancer.

One afternoon, not too long after she passed, I ran home from school, excited about something. I was oblivious to everything else as I burst through the door of our house.

"I'm home, Mom!" I shouted.

There was no sound. No movement. No smell of baking in the kitchen. Dad was working. My brothers were with their friends, I guess.

It was December of 1968. I was twelve. At that precise moment, I thought to myself, "Wow, I'm on my own."

Now, I am not going to lie. Some of my bad behavior started before my mom died. The years of her illness seem like a blur. Pain, anger, overheard late-night arguments, doctors and hospital visits — but no one ever told me what was really going on. Back then, children were to be seen and not heard. Discipline for bad behavior, which included asking questions, was usually swift.

I retreated into my mind. I lived with imaginary friends and wrote creative stories that got A's at school. At the same time, I was chastised by my teacher for daydreaming or seeking too much attention in class.

But at home, less attention was paid to me as the focus on my mother increased. When I look back at those grade-school years,

I see that I was like a pinball, bouncing from one situation to another, wanting to be noticed at any cost.

In hindsight, it seems that my need to replace my mother's love and affection after her death drove my desire to be noticed to newer and greater heights. I became fiercely competitive. I was aggressive and arrogant. I could be a braggart, a risk taker, a show-off or, sometimes, just a downright prick.

On one hand, some of this braggadocio actually generated success. I did well in sports, the social scene and business, but the early successes were, in a sense, fleeting. I might have won the prize, but I didn't win many supporters. Worse, I often spawned detractors along the way.

I remember recounting this behavior, many years back, to someone who only knew the "now" me.

He said, "Gee, it's really hard to believe that you were like that. You're such a nice guy."

"Well, thanks," I responded, with appreciation. "Maybe I wasn't really a prick deep down, but I often wore a prickly suit."

I always knew, in my heart, that inside I was a good person. Even in my young years, people who saw glimpses of that good boy told me so. I knew he was in there. It took a while, but as I got into my twenties, I started to genuinely see that the crazy lifestyle and questionable behavior were not helping me to achieve my goals.

I spent a lot of sleepless nights asking questions, praying in a sense, and looking for answers about how to let the good Phillip out and let the bad Phillip go.

It was thanks to people who encouraged me toward and rewarded me for progress along the way that I figured it out. That proved to me that you do get back what you put out, and that the universe really does conspire to deliver that which we ask for.

People I knew, and sometimes strangers, provided me with words of guidance, ideas, guidelines, and sometimes even guardrails, to help steer me along a path that kept me out of trouble or out of a casket.

Luckily, no one got injured or killed. No crimes were committed. Nothing was done that, in later years, I couldn't undo or apologize for. I was truly lucky because running along the edge of life's adventures makes it easy to slip into the abyss of tragedy. The tension between the two points of one's truth and non-truth can get so taut that something snaps. Then horrible things can happen.

So, who are you?

Are you as good a person as you're trying to make the world around you think you are?

No one is perfect. We all have secrets. What are yours?

Take a moment right now and focus in on that one thing about yourself that you most love and want the world to see.

Now, take another moment and focus in on that one thing about yourself that you most want to change.

For some of you, the journey back to self may be short. For others, it may be scary to see the gap you have created between who you truly are and what you are projecting.

In the end, the two will inevitably meet, so why not get started before something snaps?

Start small.

Visualize the end result: who you want to be and what is the response you seek from the world?

That's what worked for me and, over time, the people I needed to help me showed up to do so.

Maybe an apology to someone you have hurt could set you on the right path.

Your journey may begin with a new job or role.

Perhaps forgiving yourself for ill thoughts about others and getting on the path to seeing the good in everyone might help.

Maybe one of the 26 words in this book will be a key that unlocks you. Or perhaps your challenge is tougher, like letting go of a substance or relationship addiction and needing professional help.

There is no one more important in your life than you.

Live the life that you were meant to live from the moment you were born. When the whole world hoped the best for you. The authentic you. The real you.

You can do it. I know you can.

SIXTEEN

POOP — The answer is behind you.

"Can I call you right back?" my friend asked. "Our daughter had some blood in her poop and we're just waiting for a call from our doctor."

She later reported that they had heard back from him. "He said that if she doesn't have a fever, isn't vomiting or otherwise seeming sick, we're just to keep our eyes on her poop and watch for any changes. So there you go," she chuckled, "it's all about the poop!"

Her daughter was just about six months old and, in my opinion, the mom was getting some sound advice. Too often I have heard stories about people who get sick and then reveal that they had been having trouble pooping or peeing for months, or that they didn't think that blood in their stool was a big deal. Or that the pain when they peed was anything to worry about.

"I thought it would clear up on its own," is often what they say.

For all my male readers over fifty I ask, "Have you had a colonoscopy yet?" I am always amazed at how many men say no. Simple procedure — profound impact. As Nike would say, "Just do it."

Your body is constantly sending you signals about its condition. My norm is to feel refreshed and energized without aches, pains, itches, cramps, headaches, dizziness or blood coming out of me — from anywhere. That is not to say that I feel great every day. We all have days when we're not 100 percent.

My experience, though, has been that if I tune in to those signals and listen to my body, I can adjust accordingly, or visit my doctor if necessary.

You may have heard this saying about computers: garbage in, garbage out. Well, the same can be said of our bodies. For all the joy you may get out of doing or eating what you like, at the end of the day, there is always a reckoning. It is like your financial report card, but these are bodily signals rather than numbers.

How do you feel right now?

What does your skin look like?

How is your breathing and your sinuses?

How do your joints and muscles feel today?

How is your head functioning?

What about your sight and your hearing?

Hold your hand out in front of you. Is it steady or does it shake a bit?

How many times a day do you pee and what color is it?

How often do you poop and what is its consistency and color?

"What?" you ask. "That's gross."

When is the last time you took a good look in the toilet and inspected what is coming out of your backside?

If you continually listen to or look at the answers your body gives to these questions, you are off to a good start. If you have never even considered any of these questions, now is a good time to begin. Tune in and find out what your body is saying. You won't always like what you hear or see, but I believe that you will begin, or continue, a journey of understanding that will help you lead a healthier and, perhaps, longer life.

As with things in the rest of our lives, if your body looks, feels or seems wrong, it likely is wrong and you should seek advice on what to do. You might have to curb a certain appetite for eating, drinking, or lounging around too much!

Somewhere along my life's journey, I began to extend my visualizing to my internal self, or body. This isn't a daily process, but I do think about the journey everything takes once it enters my body. I weigh the likely benefits or harm it may bring to me as my input proceeds to being my output.

I will always remember a nurse at a blood-donor clinic telling me that they can tell if a person has recently scarfed down a greasy meal by the color of the blood. I have never confirmed that story, but it sure stuck with me.

As I write this, I am on a plane flying across Canada from Victoria, British Columbia to Toronto. The attendant just put a little dish of nuts and a glass of diet Coke on my tray. I will indulge, but I will chew the nuts thoroughly and make a mental note about this aspartame consumption, of which I'm very wary. I should be drinking water and will do so a bit later to keep hydrated.

I can tell when I listen to my body what it thinks about the stuff I am sending it, and that is a great guide for my consumption. I am a very big fan of fresh air and try to avoid breathing in the various fumes that we encounter during a day. I hold my breath when I walk by a smoker or an exhaust fan. I turn off the air conditioning in my car when I drive through smoky paving sites or when I am behind a big, diesel-powered bus. When I am out in the fresh air on a lake or in a forest, I inhale it deeply and imagine that I can store its goodness for future use.

Sometime, when you get a chance, do some reading about the thing we have all come to know as the "new car smell." Plenty has been written about the gases being given off by much of our wonderful, manufactured stuff. We seem to live in an increasingly artificially scented world. By tuning into fresh air, you will become more aware of what is going up your nose and into your lungs, which ultimately powers our bodies.

Our bodies digest each mouthful or sip of anything we ingest. I have found that the best way for me to take inventory of that is to not only listen to my body when I eat and drink, but also when I pee and poop.

Friends of ours were over for dinner last night. We discussed the fact that their young son, who was present, had swallowed a penny.

We talked about what that journey meant for him and for the penny. I shared that, when I was his age, I swallowed a marble and that a couple of days later I was playing with the same marble. He laughed at the thought.

We all know that it shouldn't hurt when we pee or that the only thing that should be coming out is water-like liquid. If mine is too yellow or concentrated, I know I need to be drinking more water. When that happens, which is only on occasion, I reflect and tend to realize that I had been feeling a bit lethargic or had a slight headache, but hadn't been paying attention.

Read up on how much water you should be drinking, but avoid excess. Having your lips glued to a bottle all day long isn't necessary. In fact, too much of anything, including water, is not the way to go. If there is pain when you pee, or something other than a liquid ranging from clear to yellow, seek a medical opinion. Early detection of any issue will always offer a better opportunity for a solution.

I heard a saying about business many years ago: If you really want to know what is going on in any business, talk to the custodians or people in the shipping and receiving department. They are the closest to what actually comes and goes from a business. Management, on the other hand, tends to talk about where a business is going. A CEO is more likely to be thinking about the next meal instead of the last one; the loading-dock staff and custodians are dealing with what was done "yesterday."

The point is that the backside of the business knows exactly what the front side of the business is up to. The same is true of our bodies. If you want to know what your mouth was up to yesterday, you only need to look behind you today and you will have a pretty good idea.

Having a nature break should be a relatively easy and somewhat pleasurable experience. Maybe that's why it's called "relieving" ourselves. If you are experiencing difficulty, start asking why. For me, too much meat or cheese, at the expense of fiber and leafy greens, is usually the culprit.

I know people who dine on fast food all the time and I can't help but wonder how their poor, embattled digestive systems handle it. "Normal" isn't feeling bloated and gassy. Normal is feeling, well — normal. I was lucky to figure that out half a lifetime ago when I was plagued by chronic sore throats and just could not seem to get healthy. I was in that period of my life where I was intoxicated with youth and being me! I recall having many tests and doctors' appointments, and perhaps some medication, prior to finally succumbing to having a gastrointestinal scan done. I remember being humbled. I had a sudden and profound realization: "This is f#@cked up."

I began analyzing my hour-to-hour and day-to-day activities with the hope of figuring out what the heck was going on, and in the end I did.

I began eating my dinner at the dinner hour instead of in the wee hours of the morning. I drank a little more water and a lot less alcohol. I started putting a tall glass of water at my bedside for sipping on. I improved my oral hygiene and made sure that my teeth and mouth were nice and clean before hitting the sack. No more flopping onto the mattress with a promise that I would brush my teeth in the morning.

All so simple and yet brilliantly effective. The sore throats stopped and my new approach to listening to my body began.

I soon started looking more closely into the toilet and I hope you do, too.

Avoid just flushing away that valuable knowledge and insight about your inner workings. Let the bowl be the crystal ball to your future health and well-being.

SEVENTEEN

PURPOSE — the magnet that draws us forward in life.

What's it all about, Alfie?
Is it just for the moment we live?
What's it all about when you sort it out, Alfie?
Are we meant to take more than we give?
Or are we meant to be kind?

This "oldie but goodie" was written in the mid-1960s by Burt Bacharach and Hal David. It was a time when the general interest in personal consciousness and awareness was burgeoning.

Just four years later, according to woodstock.com, "more than half a million people came together; united in a message of peace, openness and cultural expression — and demonstrated how a generation could be heard."

And what a generation it has been!

I was too young to attend the massive Woodstock concert, but it certainly had a seismic and historic impact on the world around me.

How many times have you asked yourself the question posed to Alfie: "What's it all about?" I ask it of myself and others regularly, especially with close friends and often in the face of life's major or mini crises.

The answer to this vital question is, to me, PURPOSE.

Prior to fairly recent generations, the purpose for most humans was driven by the need for food, shelter, warmth and clothing. It was all about survival. The world, for the most part, lived in unison with nature and had yet to create the artificial realms that we now occupy.

Certainly the class system has long existed and elevated some. People living in large cities had access to distractions from mundane questions, such as, "What is my purpose?"

Most, though, were being brought up in families that relied on the farm, were immigrants trying to survive in the new world, or perhaps returning from war to try and put the pieces of life back together.

Typically, one's purpose can be broken into two parts: what I need and what I want.

How often do you think about what you need versus what you want?

When you wake each day, do you focus on what you have or what you want to have?

Do you have a focus or are you simply responding to stimulus as it comes at you, living in "reaction" mode most of the time?

To me, for purpose to be useful and gratifying, it needs to be outside of one's self. It needs to be bigger than me or you. My experience has been that once healthy people have the food, clothing and shelter part figured out, the most rewarding purpose seems to involve helping others.

I was fortunate enough to attend a talk where the keynote speaker was economist and writer, David Foot. He spoke that day about the need for young people to have a purpose. He suggested that the lack of a purpose in youth will leave all their energy untapped, and with it they will "tear up the countries in which they live."

If you're a parent, educator or caregiver, I urge you to help the youth in your life find a purpose that will charge them up for good deeds and good lives.

In *26 Words*, I write about things that can give us forward momentum in life and this coincides with purpose. Raw momentum won't take you anywhere if you don't know where you want to go.

The wonderful thing about purpose is that it is yours to mold, adjust or change, or throw away and start again. It is intimately personal and forever completely flexible. At its most valid and fulfilling, it is positive and creates an end result that betters you, someone else, or the world around you.

Purpose is more over-arching and grander than goals, but requires setting and achieving many goals along the path to the purpose you have chosen. We can, and should, have more than one purpose because our lives are multifaceted. We are family members, community citizens, employees, teammates, friends and strangers.

Purpose is the broad statement about a general topic regarding an aspect of your life: "I want to be a parent who is loved, respected and appreciated by my children and who other children and parents look to with admiration."

There, now go tell your kids that purpose and see what they say!

As you can see, that purpose sets up a long-term journey of many goals, obstacles, joys and sorrows. But it is against that purpose that you would measure all of your actions and words. I can hear you say, "Yikes!" all the way from here, but if we look at a few more, you'll get the hang of it.

"I want to be a citizen who is seen to be making a positive contribution toward the goals and vision that has been set out by our community's civic leaders." Now, when you drive through town or walk in public, how will you behave?

"I want to be an employee who is seen to be contributing positively, at all times, to the mission of my employer. I want my fellow employees to see me as a great choice for their teams. I want other employers to compliment my employer on his good fortune having me working for them. I want to be someone who can be recommended with confidence." Now, what will you talk about at the water cooler tomorrow?

To increase the power of a statement of purpose, add why it is important to you and how it will feel pursuing that purpose, and you will have a powerful affirmation.

Here's an example.

I want to be a father who receives the love and respect of my child's mother because I make a major contribution to the efforts required to raise a child and help them along their life's course. This is important to me as a son who struggled to find his way and it will make me feel proud of the journey I have taken and obstacles I have overcome.

Such an affirmation will get you out of bed in the morning, because you will know what you need to visualize in order to move forward with, as we say, "purpose."

As George Harrison sang, "If you don't know where you're going, any road'll take you there."

The late Beatle's lyric is said to be inspired by this exchange between Alice and the wise Cheshire Cat in Lewis Carroll's Alice in Wonderland:

> *"Would you tell me, please, which way I ought to go from here?"*
>
> *"That depends a good deal on where you want to get to," said the Cat.*
>
> *"I don't much care where…" said Alice.*
>
> *"Then it doesn't matter which way you go," said the Cat.*
>
> *"…so long as I get SOMEWHERE," Alice added as an explanation.*
>
> *"Oh, you're sure to do that," said the Cat, "if you only walk long enough."*

People often ask, "So where do I start?"

"Just start," I tell them.

The answers are all around you. The instant you begin to focus on purpose in your personal and professional life, you may be quite surprised at what happens. There is a great saying, or belief, that seems to have been around for a long, long time. It is, essentially, that the universe delivers to us that which we focus upon. I have found this to be true on both the positive and negative sides of life.

When you focus on the good, good things happen. Therefore, focus on the question, "What is my purpose?" with the intent to pursue a meaningful, amazing journey. You will be astonished at what happens. People will arrive in your life with helpful clues and messages. News articles and nudges will appear. Books will jump off the shelf at you and, quite suddenly, people will see you differently. When you pursue a positive purpose, you will feel empowered because you are taking charge of you. Your worries will diminish, because you are looking at a much bigger picture. You will see more roses than thorns.

Is it easy to sustain at first?

No. Let me warn you from my experience that old attitudes, habits and beliefs die hard. Just remember that each step in a new, purposeful direction is taking you to where you want to be — not just down any old road.

One other warning: Purpose is addictive. Once you get a passion for it, you will never look back.

So the next time someone asks you, "What it's all about?" I hope you can tell them at least what it's all about for you.

EIGHTEEN

CALM — keep calm and carry on.

What are you like when pressure builds up?

Do you roll with the punches?

Do you freak out?

Do you shake and sweat?

Do you try to draw others into your drama?

It's always a choice.

"That's one choice," I have often said to friends when they are wound up about some relatively small crisis.

Some years back, I was relaxing under particularly blue skies, in the sun on my front deck, appreciating the lake. I was rolling over in my mind what the upcoming evening was going to be like.

Six months earlier, I had acquired the rights to produce a play call ART. Since then, my singular focus was to make the production one of the best my city had seen. Tonight was going to be a great night. We had pre-sold 13 shows and the buzz was strong.

ART is a three-man comedic drama about art, life and friendship. It was a long-running success on Broadway and is one of the most watched plays ever. The three stars of this production were two of my city's most talented actors and me. This was another penultimate moment in my life about to come true: I had successfully navigated (and acted) my way into a place of respect within the local theater community.

Looking back, it seemed that I was destined to do so. In Grade 10, when I told my father I had been asked to try out for the school play, he gave me an ultimatum. “You can’t play basketball at seven in the morning and then rehearse a play at seven at night and expect to do either well. You need to choose one or the other right now.”

Dad was big on ultimatums — unless you gave him one. I chose basketball.

I didn’t step on stage for the first time until the year he died, when I saw a big, yellow sign advertising acting lessons. Now a decade had passed, and ART was ready to open.

The phone rang. It was the play’s marketing director.

“Are you watching TV?”

“No. Why?”

“You need to come to my house right away.”

“Why?”

“Just come. Hurry!”

She lived just a few blocks away. When I arrived, I was rushed into the living room and was astonished to see repeat footage of two airplanes crashing into the Twin Towers in New York City.

It was 9/11.

She burst into tears. “What are we going to do?”

“Stay calm,” I replied.

If ever I’ve realized there are far bigger things to be upset about than anything in my peaceful life, it was that day.

The play ART has a wonderful scene where Ivan, a tragic, fragile man, is having a breakdown.

Serge tells Ivan to calm down. What happens next is a scene that we have all watched play out in life’s production.

“Calm down? Calm down? Don’t tell me to calm down,” Ivan retorted. “You don’t tell someone who is having a nervous breakdown to calm down!”

I had a feeling the whole country was on the verge of one.

We forced ourselves to stay calm that day. Our little troupe was emotional and overwrought by the events, but we had to consider our options. Should we cancel the opening? Should we cancel the whole production until things in New York were under control? How would a comedy look when so many people were suffering?

I took lots of deep breaths that day. I may have gone for a run. I can't remember. My mind would have explored the downside and disappointment of canceling. I would have struggled, trying to keep my personal wants and needs out of the decision-making process. I was the executive producer, so the ultimate decision was mine. A couple of hours had passed. Things were a blur. Everyone was in shock. The telephone rang.

It was Wally High, now deceased, but then actor Dan Aykroyd's best friend and head of his security.

"Hey, Phillip, listen. Danny and his crew can't make it tonight. His wife and kids are still in New York and he obviously needs to stay on top of that. He asked me to tell you that you should go ahead and re-sell his 50 tickets, if you can. I'll drop a check off later, regardless. Good luck tonight."

I had known Dan for many years and he had agreed to "buy out" half of the house on opening night. Whenever I had bumped into Dan, he had always been a big booster of my step into the acting world. When I once lamented that it was hard to make a living working, and then act on top of that, he said, "Hey, Phillip. Every actor has a day job, even me."

The production of ART was also a fundraiser for a well-known and popular veterinarian who had become a quadriplegic. It was important on the community level. "Good luck tonight," Wally had said. Dan Aykroyd's family was in the middle of a major crisis in New York, but he assumed that the show would go on, I realized.

I was heartened by this assumption from a man dealing first-hand with the crisis.

Dan had been the acting and real-life sidekick of another great comedic actor, the late and troubled John Belushi. I reckoned he had seen many a show go on despite unexpected, external challenges.

"That was Wally High," I said to my marketing manager, then explained the call. "I'm disappointed Dan isn't coming, but he assumes that the show is a go. What a guy. I hope everything is okay with his family."

We polled our team again and unanimously agreed that we could set an example — that the terrorists wouldn't get us down. In our own small way, our show could be a symbol of that to others. We drafted a note that would be ready to read at the opening of the show to explain this rationale. Then we got on the phones and were relieved to find out, when we sold those 50 tickets, that so many people agreed with our decision.

When our opening statement was read that night — just as the lights went down — the audience responded with thunderous applause.

I was waiting in the wings for my entrance and opening monologue. Tears stung my eyes.

The applause ended. I entered from behind a panel on stage left. The room was silent as the spotlight lit me. I walked toward my mark at the front of the stage. I could see our veterinarian friend in his wheelchair in the front row, smiling up at me. I walked past my mark and went quite a bit closer to the audience than I would have normally. We were all, strangely, in this thing together.

There we were after six months of producing and rehearsing the play, building the set, designing the lighting, marketing, promoting and selling all those tickets. Now, on one of the most tragic days in modern history, I stood there calmer than I could have ever imagined being. I appreciatively soaked in the audience for a few precious seconds, then began, "My friend Serge has bought a painting..."

Every day, we face people and situations that seem designed to rattle us. We have a choice about how we deal with them. We are emotional creatures and expressing emotion openly is human and healthy. It is inhumane and unhealthy when we start trying to blame someone else for how we feel or react to a situation.

You control how you respond.

Only you can make you feel.

Forget the idea that your friend, boss, co-worker, kid, partner or whoever "makes" you feel a certain way. The truth is that when anything happens, you choose to, or allow yourself to, feel a certain way and you have control of that.

It's hard, but how are you going to choose to respond to the next unwelcome event or comment?

Step back and breathe or give yourself permission to think for a moment. You have to choose your timing and your battles carefully.

Remember the story of Captain Chesley Sullenberger who miraculously landed his commercial jet in the Hudson River? He saved the lives of 155 people with the simple words, calmly spoken, "We're gonna be in the Hudson."

In other words, as the T-shirt says, "Keep calm and carry on."

NINETEEN

BEDROOM — the place of rest and love.

What is the most impactful thing you do in your bedroom?

You are wondering what I mean by that.

Let me ask again, a little differently.

What happens in your bedroom that creates the mood for the evening? Or creates the most lasting impression on your week? What sets the tone for how you sleep, wake or greet your next day?

Sometimes, the answers to questions are obvious. The answer to those questions, though, likely is not. Here is a checklist that I can guarantee will lead you to better sleep, more energy and far more positive thoughts and outlooks.

When you answer yes to a question, give yourself one point. When you answer no, give yourself zero.

IN YOUR BEDROOM, DO YOU HAVE OR DO THE FOLLOWING THINGS?	YES	NO
Television?		
Laptop or desktop computer?		
Doors or drawers open when you go to sleep?		
Lack of fresh air?		
Old sheets?		

	YES	NO
Uncomfortable mattress?		
Pillows that strain your neck?		
Abundance of artificial light?		
Discuss business?		
Argue?		
Go to sleep upset with yourself, your partner or your children?		
Sleep in some of the clothing you wore all day long?		
Hit the sack without freshening up?		
Eat in bed prior to sleeping?		
Burp, fart or breathe out foul breath while your partner is in bed with you?		
Make any noises in a bathroom close enough that your partner in bed can hear you?		
Gossip or make negative statements about people or the world around us?		
Forget to think positive thoughts about the day behind you and the one that awaits you?		
Write down your score here, if you choose, then retake this little quiz a year from now.		

Okay, so a low score is good in my non-scientific opinion. My father always said, "Never go to sleep upset." Yours probably did, too. But the importance of that advice cannot be overstated. We need a calming place to help us divest ourselves of the harried world, with all of its frenetic energy surging through our bodies, minds and souls.

I strongly believe that our bedrooms need to be controlled places that offer a reprieve and refresher from everything around us. An oasis, if you will.

I believe that we can improve our lives and health immensely by changing our bedrooms to be places of warmth and tranquility. It is the place where we can rest and form images of a wonderful life. It is a place where we should feel relaxed and refreshed. It is a place where we can hide from the world and heal a nasty cold. It is a place where even the greatest of most powerful men and women can, and hopefully do, have a good pillow fight or giggle at something silly.

I know that this will not be an easy task for some of you. Old habits die hard.

The things of false comfort and distraction that have crept into our bedrooms are not purged easily. Televisions and computers have, for some, become tools to prevent introspection at the most critical time of the day. It takes time to adjust to a bedroom void of energy-sucking technology. It is so worth it, though.

Recently, for very pragmatic reasons, I reluctantly installed a wall-hung flat panel television in one corner of my bedroom.

When I travel on business, I seem to always fall into the trap of turning on that darn TV that beckons at the end of the bed. Most nights it keeps me up later than I want as I flick through the channels to realize, again, that there is nothing worth watching. With heavy eyelids, I finally drop the controller and kill the lights.

Our house was busy one night and I needed some alone time. "Ah ha," I thought, "I now have a TV upstairs in the bedroom."

The next morning, my wife told me that when she came to bed, I was sound asleep, television on and remote in hand.

"Argh! Never again!"

I made a decision that if I watch television in our room, I will sit in a chair as opposed to lying in bed. That makes the action more deliberate.

I leave the television unplugged so it is not 'alive' when I am sleeping.

Furthermore, if you were to walk into our room and look around you would not see a television.

What you would see in the corner would be a beautiful 24"x36" color photo of one of my favorite places in the world. I had it blown up and mounted on foam core with a couple of Velcro tabs stuck to the back. It covers the television until I need to watch it.

I am proud of that compromise and accomplishment that helps me live what I am writing about and still meet my need for that darn device.

Here's another thing that might seem odd at first: never argue in the bedroom. Yes, asking your partner to leave the comfort of warm sheets and blankets to discuss this or that in another part of the house may not be embraced. I wish my parents had done that when they had the odd scrap. Yes, my father said, "Never go to bed angry," but we all know the doing is harder than the saying.

I have worked diligently on this one and it has paid big dividends. Most of what is bugging me can usually be resolved internally, and the idea of having to get out of bed to resolve conflicts can be a good incentive to decide how important a matter really is before broaching it in the middle of the night.

From my experience, though, taking an issue out of the bedroom to be discussed elsewhere accomplishes several things. Things tend to be resolved faster, I think, because you are honoring each other and a respectful process. You will both feel much better about each other. The trek back to the bedroom will be a joyful one, may bring out some of those giggles and, yes, it could well lead to one of the healthy activities bedrooms are meant for.

I am not sure what brain chemicals get activated in that process, but I sure enjoy them!

Additionally, I think that when we do slip into the sheets, they should be crisp, clean linen on an awesome bed, with welcoming pillows. There should be no excuse for uncomfortable, permanently rumpled or dirty bedding.

After all, most of us spend one third of our lives in bed. Yet, for many, a great bedroom set seems to be the last thing they will spend money on. A new car, boat, lawnmower, snow blower, patio set, pool...why do other things take precedence?

My first real career was establishing a chain of waterbed stores when waterbeds were offering a comfort level not then achieved by standard mattresses. While the waterbed has long since morphed into new technology, its impact on comfortable sleeping surfaces will last forever. Today, there is a bed, linen and pillow for even the pickiest and most discerning sleeper.

If all this bedroom talk is creating a new or renewed enthusiasm in you, and you want to really get into it, I have two words for you: Feng shui.

There are many wonderful books and articles on Feng shui, which has been around for thousands of years.

I agree with the Wikipedia definition: at its essence, Feng shui is a "philosophical system of harmonizing the human existence with our surrounding environment." In other words, it helps humans figure out how we can best get with our physical surroundings.

You might want to do a bit of quick research now, then come back to do a quick scorecard to see how your bedroom fares against the Feng shui criteria.

Regardless, I urge you to reassess your bedroom attributes, attitudes and behaviors and decide if there is room for improvement.

Go to bed every night with the mental image that it's your first day on holiday or one of the best times you had sharing the bed with your partner.

Set the bar high everywhere in life — and that includes your bedroom.

TWENTY

COURTESY — the coin of kings.

When is the last time some small gesture from a friend or stranger made your day?

I have been told that courtesy is the coin of kings.

So what does that mean, really?

I remember my first trip to Vancouver, British Columbia. I was staying with a friend at his apartment in the Kitsilano Beach area. Late one afternoon, I went for a walk to explore the neighborhood and ended up having to cross West Broadway Street. It was a very busy four-lane road and this was the evening drive-home time. I looked both ways, assessing the volume of traffic, and then stepped off of the curb to get a better look. The strangest thing happened: the cars in both directions stopped.

It took me more than a few seconds to realize that they had stopped to let me cross the street safely. "Wow," I thought. "Back home, people would rather run me over or scare the beejeepers out of me with their horns than slow down, let alone stop!"

Talk about courtesy making an impression.

Many years ago, I attended a funeral at a small, rural funeral home in farming country, north of my hometown. The deceased was a close relative of a long-term employee of our business. My brother and I were there to show our support during this time of grief. The home was packed with neighbors, friends, family and acquaintances of the deceased. It was a casual, yet respectful, gathering of people who came to share the celebration of a life well spent.

We gathered in the chapel for the formal and informal eulogies. Due to my emotional distance from the deceased, I was present but sometimes absent at the same time. My mind was wandering over a plethora of topics.

This sort of distraction, or daydreaming, is a challenge for many as we miss the opportunity to fully immerse ourselves in any one experience. I was regularly chastised as a young school boy for "day-dreaming out the window," as my teachers called it.

To this day, focus remains a challenge as my busy mind tries to lead me off in many directions.

I am aware now of this tendency and am better able to pull myself back to the moment. Moments that allow me to be courteous, rather than appear uninterested or, worse, rude.

It was a lovely, sunny day in the late fall, and my brother and I chose to follow the funeral procession to the cemetery. A long string of cars slowly meandered down the picturesque, narrow, country road.

As we exited the light grasp of the small town, we followed the cortege and proceeded out into the countryside. I enjoyed the vista over the plowed fields.

I watched as a farmer stopped his tractor and dismounted onto the freshly turned soil. He removed his hat and mopped his beaded brow while he stared toward our stream of cars. A few hundred yards along, on the opposite side of the road, I viewed a similar scene. Again and again, men on tractors came to a halt, dismounted, put their work aside, removed their hats and watched the funeral procession pass.

My eyes moistened. My heart swelled. I was witnessing a simple, yet so poignant, gesture of respect and courtesy. These people, who continually fight time to harvest the bounty of nature, had literally stopped in their tracks to pay their respect to someone they may not even have known.

"Will anyone stop what they're doing when my hearse passes?" I wondered. "Wouldn't that be nice?"

In Canada, a tradition took root when the bodies of fallen Canadian soldiers, who had lost their lives in Afghanistan, were transported along Highway 401 in a funeral cortege from the military base in Trenton, Ontario to the coroner's office in downtown Toronto, Ontario.

For the first time this thoroughfare, which was named the Highway of Heroes, offered citizens an opportunity to show their respect and appreciation by lining the route and the overpasses above it. They were somber, grateful witnesses to processions of families, military, police and funeral officials in black vehicles accompanying brave, young men and women on their final journeys.

The outpouring of support was tremendous. Thousands of people, of all generations, turned out in every sort of weather to stand silently, cheer wildly, wave flags or hold placards high in hands tiny and large. Fire trucks and other emergency vehicles would often join the trip to the local overpass, with red lights spinning and blinking.

My business driving regularly takes me along the highway that these processions traveled. It takes under two minutes for the collection of vehicles to pass on the opposite side of the wide, divided highway. I have pulled over to the side of the road three times to watch the cortege pass and to say a silent prayer.

I feel that was a unique opportunity in life to express appreciation and respect for those who fought for freedom.

I now make a point of pulling over whenever any funeral passes by.

Like those farmers in the fields who inspired me years earlier, I, luckily, made it to a place in life where I know that "time well given is time well spent." I have come to understand that the giving of my time is truly the greatest courtesy I can offer in some situations.

Courtesy in our personal and intimate relationships is truly the gold currency that keeps the economy of that relationship growing.

Why is it so easy to be discourteous with the people we love the most?

What happens to all the niceties and gentle acts of kindness that attract people to each other? Why do they somehow fade to a distant memory to be replaced by presumption, or worse, lack of respect?

I make a conscious effort to be courteous with people in general, people I care about and, in particular, people I love. It wasn't always that way when, as a younger person, I almost took pride in just the opposite in many personal relationships.

Most of the biggest fights with my brothers were instigated through an absence of courtesy.

I still make lots of mistakes, but always correct my course quickly with actions and words.

How courteous are you?

When is the last time you turned on your courtesy meter and measured?

What would it read these days?

Do you build up your partner and loved ones with your words?

Do you compliment them in front of others?

How hard is it to say, "I love you. I am proud of you. I appreciate you," to those you love?

Courteous words are a healing tonic. If you have not used them in a while, get back to it and feel the heal.

It was a hard transition for me, but now I am addicted to the great feeling that comes from simply being courteous.

Courtesy runs in the simplest deeds as well.

It's as easy as "you before me" or "I cut, you choose." A simple gesture, like a thank-you card sent by snail mail after a party or special dinner, will be warmly remembered months after any event.

Have you been the "victim" of a random act of kindness?

I was the grateful recipient of a shining example of random courtesy. A few days after my brother passed on, there was a sudden, loud knock at my door. Where I live, people generally call before they drop by because my house is a little out of the way. I was alone at the time and wondered who on earth it could possibly be.

I opened the door to one of the shyest, warmest smiles ever.

"It must be awful," he said. "I can't imagine."

I knew this big, larger-than-life man professionally, but not that well personally. He proceeded to give me a bear hug in the doorway.

"I just wanted to give you a big hug and say it will be okay. That's all." He pulled back, looked into my eyes, squeezed my shoulders encouragingly, and then turned to leave.

I closed the door and watched him drive away. Tears flooded my eyes. I think I actually said aloud, "Wow."

I drop into wakes and funerals, send cards and make calls to people I know — sometimes even peripherally — because I have learned through experiences like that one how powerful such a gesture is in times of need.

You can open a door, assist your neighbor, let a walker cross a busy road, hold your partner's hand, help someone with directions or simply smile at strangers and wish others a good day when you're out on a walk.

That last one always makes me smile. I love seeing how initially surprised people are when I say, "Good morning," and how pleased they are once they realize that a stranger is just passing on a courtesy.

Simple acts of courtesy often say more than any words ever can.

Sound too easy?

Just watch world leaders or royalty or dignitaries on television. They go to great pains to allow the other to go first or sit first or say the first words. At that unique, high level of accomplishment, what else do they have but courtesy to offer their peers?

Hmm. Maybe that's why courtesy is sometimes viewed as being the coin of kings.

But there's no reason you and I can't make it our daily tender, too.

TWENTY-ONE

GROW — to grow, you must let go.

When is the last time you did something that you never thought you could or would do?

Over the course of a summer, many years back, I had long discussions with a friend about the damaged relationship she had with her father. She was in her late twenties then.

Her dad had abandoned her as a young girl and then re-appeared, sometime around her eighteenth birthday, hoping for a warm welcome from her and her mom. Grudgingly, my friend let him back into her life. The pain and anger she was carrying became more evident as our conversations deepened. She ran the full gamut of anger, sadness, and sometimes even laughter, at how stupid it all was.

Some days, she would be visibly shaking after one of our discussions. I did my best to listen, but I really did want to "fix" her. I explored the ideas of hope and forgiveness with her and the notion that our entire society is based on those two social concepts.

We hope for the best in each other each day.

We have simple and complex systems of forgiveness for those who let us down.

"Okay, fine," she said one day. "I guess I can forgive him and move on." There was a pause as she took a long draw from her cigarette and gazed at me with piercing eyes. "But I will never forget what he did!"

What are you carrying in your heart and soul that is gnawing at you? What do you wake up thinking about in the middle of the night or tell your friends about until they finally remind you that they have heard it all before?

Do you brood about how your parents, a friend, co-worker, employer, neighbor, child, sibling or mere acquaintance treats or treated you?

Are you so full of old issues that there is no room for the new and positive?

Did you lock onto something that, no matter what, you are not letting go of?

Not long ago, I was driving a friend's pickup truck. It was a lovely, sunny Sunday early in the day when I pulled into the parking lot of our local Home Depot store. I swung the truck lazily into one of the many open parking spaces.

I hadn't realized that a small car was following until he pulled up on the passenger side and parked right beside me. His proximity to my truck made it difficult for him to get out of his car. He threw me a look to let me know that he was annoyed.

I thought nothing of it, exited the truck, clicked the lock on the key fob, and headed to the store.

"Nice f*$@ing parking job!" he yelled at me.

It was about 8:30 in the morning. There were very few cars in the 1,000-space parking lot and ample room for both of us. I looked over my shoulder at a man, about 5'10", clean-cut, reasonably well-dressed. Could have been a professional of some sort. "Pardon?"

He pointed back at my parking spot.

"I said nice f*$@ing parking job. Can't you see the lines?"

He was right. I was over the line by about a foot. I usually don't drive a truck and, anyway, "big deal," I thought. There were dozens and dozens of empty spots all around us.

What you are about to read is not a recommended approach, but I will share it as, shall we say, a learning exercise.

The man and I were about twenty feet apart. I live in a small town and, within one degree of separation, would certainly be connected to this person.

"Sorry, it's a borrowed truck. Not used to it," I told him, to assure him that I hadn't parked that way to annoy him. I assumed he would understand. I assumed wrong.

"Yeah, right. Well, learn how to drive then," or something to that effect, was his contemptuous response. He strode past me toward the store. Here comes the not-recommended part.

"That must be really heavy," I called to his back.

He stopped and turned.

"Uh, oh," I thought. "Jeez, Phillip, you have a big mouth."

"What are you talking about?" he demanded.

"That baggage you're hauling around. It must be really heavy."

"F*$@ you," he spat and, luckily for me, stomped away.

That was bad behavior on my part. My father always said, "Never tangle with someone who has less to lose than you do."

My actions could have backfired. It could easily have ended up in a bad situation. Yes, that Sunday we were both wrong. The difference is that I had clarity of mind. I knew better the moment I mouthed off, but the situation goaded me into bad behavior. I let my instinct, instead of my knowledge, take over.

We must do our best to always avoid the temptation that arises when someone else's behavior is bad. Lots of people really are having personal struggles we can't see just by looking at them. Plus, you might just get punched in the face if you tangle with the wrong person on the wrong day.

Behavior rarely correlates to its appearance.

Someone who steals isn't necessarily a thief at heart.

Someone who is grumpy at work all day isn't necessarily the jerk they appear to be.

Someone who behaves badly is rarely a bad person.

I assessed the man in the parking lot as someone who was harboring a grudge — or carrying a bag of them — and was lashing out at me because he was at the boiling point and couldn't contain himself. For a reasonable-looking guy, it seemed that he was just itching to pull whoever he could into his darkness.

For all I know, he had just received some truly tragic news. I somehow doubt it, though. It struck me as more deep-seated than that. It appeared that he was so blinded by his burdened soul that he couldn't see how ridiculous his behavior was. He couldn't hold back, for even one second, to wonder who we might know in common in our smallish city.

Have you ever been annoyed at a driver and honked, only to discover it was someone you knew?

I have and it's embarrassing.

Behavior is like a weed or plant, a bush or tall tree. It always has a root.

Our job is to assess our attitudes, habits and beliefs, and determine if they are connected to healthy and life-giving roots or immersed in the toxic soil of our inability to forgive.

You are reading this book, so it strikes me as highly likely that you are, more or less, functioning reasonably well in life and society.

I think that the bitter man in the parking lot may have needed a counselor, not a book.

Sometimes, we're not aware of our behavior or the impact it has on those around us. As you read, you may be recognizing some of the symptoms that arise from harboring ill feelings in yourself.

If you want to get to the next level and let go of old baggage, you can. Here is a little surprise for you: it doesn't involve anyone else at all. The baggage we carry is usually baggage about ourselves!

Here are some simple questions to help you start unpacking:

- What's in your heart and weighing on your soul right now?
- Who is the one family member who pulls negativity out of you as a result of something in the past?
- Who is the one friend you need to reconcile with to let go of an old grudge?
- What is it about your work that drives you bonkers, and what can you do about it?
- What is the one emotional quality about yourself that you would like to change?
- What is the one physical quality about yourself that you would like to change?

There are six starting points for you. Now, get out some paper and start writing, or open up your computer and start typing. Capture everything you can think of about at least one of those questions. Be open and honest; this is for your eyes only, to get to know yourself.

This simple exercise will help you let go, so you can grow.

TWENTY-TWO

ATTITUDE — increases our altitude.

What was your attitude about the world around you today?

Or yesterday?

Or last week?

Or over the last year?

Are you seeing the thorns or the roses?

Is it the gray clouds on the horizon that capture your attention?

Does that thing that your friend, co-worker or family member said to you angrily claw at the back of your mind?

Can you let go of the runway and, like an airplane, pull your nose up, increase your positive attitude and gain altitude in your life, relationships, job, health and soul?

Airlines have baggage limits and so should you.

How much stuff are you going to carry on your flight of life?

What are you going to carry on and what are you going to check?

It is your choice.

Let's do something together right now, okay?

Think of some small thing that you have been carrying in your heart for many years.

It could be a comment made to you by a friend, family member or stranger. It could have been a situation where you felt upstaged. It could have been something more traumatic, like a loss or injury, and I express my sympathy to you for that.

Now, take a deep breath and say aloud, "I acknowledge that which happened to me and I am now ready to let it go."

"Let it go" are three of the other most powerful words in personal and professional growth.

Or, more harshly put, we have to "get over it."

Sorry to simplify things and hold you accountable for you, however, that is what we are talking about here. Learning about yourself is why you are reading this book.

So, can you let it go?

Will you?

Start with something small and grow from there.

I can't do it for you, but I can share that it works. Like a hot-air balloon that drops a weight over the side, I know that you will rise with every affirmation you make to yourself to let go of something that is holding you down.

I was chatting with a dear friend recently. She is a born worrier and over-thinker, and I was trying to help her focus on the positive. She wears her emotions on her sleeve and she sometimes lets life get her down. She can remember all the negatives in her life, and often that masks the fact that she actually leads a truly blessed life.

Does that sound familiar?

There are lots of sayings about focusing on that which we can control and letting go of that which we can't. That's a common thread through these 26 words.

It is easy to get sucked into a downward swirl, especially with the proliferation of the media and their endless hours of drama — much of the time about nothing, or speculation. Even the weather channels, with almost constant warnings or footage of natural disasters, are into worst-case scenarios that keep people amped up about what might happen. We all have the power, each moment of each day, to unplug or unglue ourselves from the negative and choose to be positive.

Part of the process of discovery and actualizing this approach to a positive attitude is the need for reflection or silence, which I talked about a few chapters ago.

It is important to look at and listen to ourselves on an ongoing basis.

If you are trying to improve your attitude, start by measuring its current state.

If this is all new to you, try reflecting on the last thirty minutes or hour as a start. How did you respond to the world and people around you?

I have worked hard since my time in Africa to see and seek the positive. That effort influences my attitude in a dramatic way.

I generally try to avoid the news or, more specifically, the graphic images that are so often used to shock us. Don't get me wrong; I am not out of touch. It's just that nine times out of ten, I can get most of the dramatic story from the headlines and lead paragraph, without immersing myself in it.

I can't turn the light on for you, but I can tell you that there is a switch within each of us that says "positive" or "negative." All we need to do is acknowledge that switch and flick it to positive.

One generous judgment at a time. You can do it.

We are not aiming for perfection. I work at being positive every moment of every day, in the face of every circumstance. It's an ongoing struggle, so I applaud myself internally for each attitude-adjusting minute, moment or circumstance I master. I know you can, too.

When you decide to go from bad attitude to good, you are going to face some interesting responses. People who knew you and liked your dark side may not feel the same or relate to you as well. Many of my old friends are no longer in my life, because when I really looked at what bound us together, it was not something sustainable — such as a hopeful view of the world around us.

Change is hard enough on the inside and even harder when the outside resists it as well.

Don't worry if some of your old colleagues start calling you Goodie Two Shoes. They will either come around or recede into the distance as you gain personal and, probably, professional altitude.

You will be awed by who you meet and what you experience on your new journey.

In the world of magnets, positive attracts negative.

In the world of attitude, positive attracts positive.

One of the most important tools that helps me find an opportunity for positivity in every situation is the all important "pause." Yes, think before you speak. Take that breath before you engage.

Life is coming at us at a rapid pace and we are under intense demands to deal with a multitude of circumstances on a daily basis.

It's often easier to default to that old negative attitude instead of a new positive one. But we can't let the negative keep us grounded with wheels on the pavement instead of soaring high above.

Often what pulls at our negative attitudes is rooted in poor communication or lack of consideration from people around us.

Even in the face of extremely challenging times, we have a choice as to how we allow that circumstance to affect us. It is often easy to react negatively and blame others for that choice.

Here's an idea: the next time you think something derogatory about someone else, try replacing their name with your own. We do dislike in others what we dislike in ourselves!

My late brother used a great example in meetings where those present started bad-mouthing someone who wasn't.

"Hold on a second," he'd say, then get up and change seats to pretend to be the absent person. "Okay, I am so-and-so now, and have just arrived at the meeting. Go ahead and continue the conversation."

I bet you can imagine how the dynamic changed. Simple gesture — powerful impact.

Often when we criticize others, we are really speaking to ourselves about ourselves, or trying to increase our own altitude by putting others down below us.

That is a poor way to climb, let alone soar.

We can't do anything about the past, but we sure can do something about the future, referring to the past only as a guide or measuring stick. Your next opportunity to choose a better attitude and gain positive altitude in life is coming soon.

Are you ready to take flight?

TWENTY-THREE

TRUTH — will set you free.

Have you ever slipped down that slippery slope with one small untruth leading to another...and another... until you are really in the drink and not sure how to fess up?

It is so easy to do. After all, each day we are faced with opportunities to gild the truth or, worse, lie outright.

As a young, hurt boy, I added to my list of undesirable traits the one of being a braggart. I exaggerated to try and make myself look better in front of others. I enhanced my stories and sought to one-up other people's so I could get the attention.

I have to admit that this is a quality that dies very hard. While I have long since learned the value of truth, transparency and facts, I still feel a slight urge, on occasion, to sprinkle the facts with a bit of glitter.

Maybe it's my overactive imagination. Maybe it's my desire to please or persuade, or maybe it's just a hangover from a bad habit long since vanquished. I do know that it is not motivated by the same desire to be noticed that it was when I was young. There is no ill intent in my glitter dust.

Maybe I am just overly enthusiastic, so I am always fact-checking mentally now when I talk or share a story.

Like a bubble in water, the truth always surfaces. When it does reveal itself, it can diminish your reputation, or even cause pain or grief, if you have betrayed it.

The good news is that, when handled with love and care, the truth really can set you free.

A friend of mine was lying on his bed reading a book. He heard the sound of his wife crying in their en suite bathroom. He called out, "Honey, are you okay?"

Yes, a wiser man would have gotten up to check in person, but my friend did not. They had just joyously given birth to their second child; what could the problem be?

"How can you possibly love me when I look the way I do?" she sobbed.

My friend deduced that his wife, fresh from the shower, was probably standing naked in front of the brightly lit bathroom mirror.

There was a long silence.

Perspiration stung his armpits.

He took a deep breath.

"There is no correct answer to that question," he replied.

Silence.

"I love you," she finally said, in a calmer voice.

"I love you too, darling. Can I get you anything?"

"No, that's fine. I'm just getting dressed."

Before you blast my friend for being a dolt, you need to know that he and his wife were, at the time, very popular stage actors who specialized in farce. This could have easily been a scene from one of their plays.

Sometimes we get put in a corner when the truth does need to be tempered with judgment. In this case, had he said, "In my eyes, you look beautiful," it would have been 100 percent true. Given their relationship, he used humor to ease his way out of what could have been a tight corner. You see, truth for truth's sake is rarely a good option.

How many of us have been confronted with this dreaded question: "Do I look fat in these jeans?"

We know what we should say. "I am just telling you the truth," is not an appropriate disclaimer for being an insensitive idiot.

The next time you are asked a question that may require a truthful answer that could be hurtful, try this. Take two long breaths and let your heart, not your brain, put the words in your mouth. When you speak, be sure what you say is fair for all concerned at that time.

A good guide in life is assuming that the truth will always surface with any of our actions and behaviors and acting accordingly.

The notion of truth as a catalyst for personal freedom is absolutely valid. It is so easy, though, to go through life racking up a long list of deceptions with our friends, our employers, our family, our community and, most importantly, ourselves.

In a perfect world, even minor untruths would be easily avoided. Our world is not perfect, and occasionally a "white lie" does make it more palatable.

Too often, though, lies are spun purely for convenience or as a means to an end. Those moments can easily gain momentum.

And then they catch up with us.

Truth and life always reconcile.

Truth can be the greatest building block of a wonderful life. Deception can wreak havoc on once-solid relationships, spirit and health.

That is not to say that one always needs to rush forth and make admissions.

We have three choices:

1) maintain an honest, high-integrity approach throughout your relationships with others,
2) ignore the fact that you have been filling a bag up with small, medium and potentially large deceptions, or

3) get busy being truthful with yourself and those around you, and stay that way.

Getting bitten by the second approach usually brings about the first, but it is the third that will create true wisdom within you.

So, where does one start?

Well, you have three types of relationships in your life: personal, professional, and with yourself and whatever spirit or faith that entails.

I suggest that you start with yourself first because being true to yourself will make it infinitely easier to be authentic with others.

What are the things that you perpetually lie to yourself about?

It might sound harsh, but we all do it.

How do you truly feel about yourself? Your body? Your mind? Your soul? Your relationship with the world around you, both natural and manmade? Your connections with friends, family, peers and workmates? Your relationship with food, vices or addictive substances?

Begin with what works for you. The thoughts in your mind have to translate into action.

Write to yourself, talk to a trusted friend, join a blog community, or seek counseling to discuss things from your past or present that you need to start being truthful about.

Truth for truth's sake won't set you free, but a heartfelt approach with yourself and those around you will.

I bet many of you can recall situations where you have lied to get around some sticky situation. It's never too late to revisit a moment like that and come clean with the people you lied to.

Mind you, you must approach that gently and give serious thought to the outcome. Rushing back and heaping honesty on surprised recipients for your own selfish reasons is unlikely to create a positive end result.

Will your admission be a relationship building block of equal value to both parties if you take this route?

Perhaps it helps to break it down into two types of untruth: animate and inanimate.

Inanimate moments or events have to do with things. Maybe you took, broke, lost, damaged or otherwise diminished the value of an item, and then made up a story to cover your tracks.

Confessing to your brother that it was you who, five years ago, scraped the bumper of his sports car would likely be the sort of thing that would be good to clear up.

To me, though, animate moments or events are the personal or very hurtful ones. If you blamed someone else for your brother's car damage, well, that really must be cleared up.

Animate moments abound: cheating on someone; failing to show for an important gathering; conspiring against others; handling money badly; creating issues of bad health; breaking commitments or promises to your children, friends, relatives and peers…

This is sticky stuff and needs to be handled delicately, depending on the degree of impact on others.

Distance, time and ultimate outcomes can mean that admitting to something today won't mean as much as it would have then. But time does not heal all wounds, as we know.

Telling your brother, now happily married with great kids and a good life, that you did indeed sleep with his girlfriend in high school might just clear up a family mystery between the two of you. Everyone might even have a good chuckle over it. However, I can't guarantee that because I don't know your brother and he may still want to take a swing at you.

Over the years, our business has received letters and checks from ex-employees acknowledging theft and seeking forgiveness. To me, that is pretty cool and a great sign for that person's future.

This is about you taking personal responsibility for being less than truthful and acknowledging that in a pure way to yourself, first of all, without rationalizations or justifications.

Then and only then should you come clean with someone in a way that will truly be a building block for a better relationship, not a cause of further damage. Sometimes, we just have to live with guilt and take it as a lesson that will help us in the future.

Always keep the impact on others in the forefront of your words and actions.

For some, this journey will be daunting. For others, it may affirm being on the right track. What matters is that you set a goal of personal and professional honesty and integrity and work toward it within yourself. Each step of the way will be rewarding.

Start slowly.

Make lasting and sustainable steps.

There is no one, simple answer for all. The fact is that the mere exercise of focusing on these questions will bring answers, and relief and joy, in the process. I have heard it said that, "We bring upon ourselves that which we focus upon."

May I suggest that a focus on truth is a pretty good bet?

TWENTY-FOUR

CHANGE — it's happening all around you.

How often have you struggled and struggled with a decision to make a major or minor change in your life? Then, when you finally made the decision, you felt a huge weight lift off your soul. You asked yourself and friends, "Why did I wait so long to do that?" You found yourself saying, "I can't believe how much better I feel, now that I have made that decision."

This phenomenon seems to be particularly evident when it comes to leaving bad relationships. We may have gotten so used to a certain circumstance that we can't imagine life any other way. We stay, even though we are in emotional turmoil or pain, paralyzed by fear of the unknown. Could it be worse?

For some reason, we humans seem to be programmed to resist improvement — yet existence as a society shows just the opposite. Everything around us is constantly changing and evolving, but we resist, rather than embrace, shifts and transformations — even small ones.

Consider the miracle of birth and growth.

From the moment of conception, we are in a continuous process of change, renewal and growth. Our very first cell needs to break in half to become two cells. That process, of course, happens throughout our gestation. Then we must exit the warmth of the womb and enter a strange, new world. We are severed from the life-giving umbilical cord, thrust into the glare of harsh lights, and often have our airways suctioned to get us breathing properly.

Imagine how scary it would be if we were conscious of that process. I think we would resist leaving our warm, soothing water-world every step of the way.

It doesn't get a lot better when we enter the world. Just as we get comfortable as a suckling child, we are moved from the breast and onto a bottle or sippy cup. Then comes the cold spoon forcing food into our mouth.

Soon we can't even pee or poop in our convenient, soft diaper. We have to be trained to climb onto a plastic potty. Then, just when that gets working, we are asked to up the ante and climb onto a cold porcelain monster.

More change. More letting go of what we once found comforting.

Soon, like the tiny bird gently nudged from the nest and forced to fly or die, we little ones are sent from home to new buildings with new people that all at once scare, challenge, excite, teach and stimulate us.

Suddenly, we're little people who now have to make choices every moment of every day for the rest of our lives. Do we resist change later in life because we are forced to change so much, so early in life?

Those first years are not comprised of changes we choose to make. They are initiated by people and forces beyond our control. Maybe that explains why change is challenging for us. Maybe we are hard-wired to resent it.

Once we become independent adults, we face a new challenge to learn how to initiate change within ourselves, or to motivate others to change.

It is worth taking a moment to talk about the three stages of change: denial, acknowledgment and acceptance. I have found that these three stages are inevitable. Knowing about them has been a tremendous help when I have faced large or small changes in my life.

Denial is that time when you just can't accept that change is happening. You are angry and refuse to even consider the change you are facing. You may feel depressed, lethargic, unmotivated and short-tempered. You may be sleeping poorly, or even feel ill, as you absorb that the change is real. Denial is so intense that I've found it can only be sustained for a while. My observation about how long most people can blind themselves to what the rest of the world sees is a few weeks or months. People in longer periods of severe denial likely should seek the opinion of a professional.

The second stage, acknowledgment, seems to be far more absorbing and can last many months or even years. In some cases, people drag their ill feelings about having to acknowledge a change to their grave. Dragging that anvil of resistance too long or far may actually lead them to death sooner.

Acknowledgment is sort of like calling "Timber!" as the tree falls. The cutting is done. The inevitable is now obvious. There is now no denying that change is upon you as you watch what was once tall and strong in your life, mind or soul fall at your feet.

"Fine!" you say. "Maybe it happened, I can't stop it, but I am not happy and I am not going to adjust or accept it."

Have you ever been there?

How long did you resist?

How much ill will did it cause you and those around you?

Was it the loss of a relationship, job, asset, friend or perhaps even a part of your body?

Here is where I will share three of the most powerful words I know that promote personal and professional growth.

Get over it!

In my public talks, I use "let it go" because "get over it" can seem a little harsh. At the end of the day, though, "get over it" is what your friends and family really want to say to you.

"Get over it and move on. You'll be fine. We love you. We are here for you."

Getting over something, or letting go, allows you to enter the stage of grace that almost always arrives: acceptance. I say "almost" in case you are one who does decide to drag the anvil of spite right to your early grave.

Acceptance is that morning when you rise and the veil has lifted. You feel light of heart and soul. Something is different. You wonder what it is.

It is you!

You are back, so to speak.

You never actually went anywhere. You just took yourself, friends, family and peers on a journey through the three stages of change.

They all notice your lighter mood and step immediately. Inevitably, you will ask them, "Why didn't you tell me to get over it?" They will usually reply that they did.

Have you been there? I have.

Understanding the change process can help you accelerate through it, get on with life and minimize the damage.

We see examples of accelerated acceptance all the time when people who have faced trauma emerge to become inspirations as they share how they survived or overcame a tragedy.

Change can strike in a frightening or heart-breaking instant.

In that case, we have no time for preparedness. Change is thrust upon us in an instant — a telephone call, a confrontation, an accident, a coincidence or a close call.

We have no choice but to face and handle those blink-of-an-eye situations. There can be no denial. We work through it because there is no option, though it often results in shock or depression later, as the reality settles in. Longer-term change can take days, months or years as one struggles with something deeply rooted such as an addiction, abusive situation, broken relationship or family dysfunction.

I have faced sudden loss in my life. Through my business, I get situations that surprise me daily. In my life of travel, sports and adventure, I have been on the edge of disaster more times than I care to share.

Some of the hardest changes I have made, though, are around circumstances that I have been immersed in for some time — the ones that I have been enduring and have had lots of time to brood about; the changes that create gut-wrenching fear about what may be on the other side; the changes that, when contemplated, wake me from my deepest sleeps.

I have worked hard to embrace change. That doesn't mean it's easy. Some have to "get over it"; I just "get at it." I move into the difficult situations quickly and get on with it. I have seen the power of change in my life bring bounty beyond my dreams. I have come to know that all of us ultimately have to face situations that need change. There is no escaping it.

What I focus on is the desired end result.

I visualize the positive outcome.

I discuss with friends or advisers what I am contemplating.

I try to pick the right place and time, and then I wade in.

I have learned to move through denial and acknowledgement like obstacles to the ribbon at the finish line of acceptance. I keep my eye on the prize and try to listen carefully to my wise inner bird about why I am being challenged with a given situation.

It hurts to grow. That's just the way it is.

The sapling that doesn't shed its bark and reach to the sun will be overwhelmed by the very tree and forest that gave it life.

The snake that fails to scrape itself against a sharp rock to shed its skin will be suffocated by the casing that once gave it life.

For humans, it's often hard to realize that the only thing holding us back from changing and growing is ourselves. Look in the mirror and ask yourself what you want to be, or where you want to be, or who you want to be. Then reflect for a moment on the biggest obstacle to you becoming you.

If you stretch, you will grow. It hurts, but the joys of change and growth are balms for the soul that eventually, or quickly, ease our pain.

TWENTY-FIVE

PRESENCE — just show up.

How did you feel the last time someone kept you waiting, or worse, stood you up?

There is a quote, often attributed to Woody Allen, that, "Eighty percent of life is just about showing up." Is it as simple as that?

My late father, a consummate entrepreneur, would say to my two brothers who worked for him early in their careers, "If you have a &@%$ing problem, don't write a &@%$ing letter or make a &@%$ing telephone call. Get in your &@%$ing car and show up!"

Despite the fact that Dad liked to pepper his teachings with profanity, he did pass on some great lessons. Yes, the other twenty percent — what you bring to the table when you do show up — is extremely important. But I have to say, my Dad's and Woody's point seems even more relevant in today's social-media-fueled world.

Creating enduring relationships and a sustainable solution for a problem involving other people is, and I believe always will be, done best in person. We seem hard-wired to interact face to face; the true measure of a person can best be taken when your eyes meet theirs. Electronic communication is great once the relationship is firmly established. Until then, though, in-person is paramount.

Why do you think our world leaders fly around the globe to meet in person? The United Nations could just host a conference call or Skype and save all that money. It could easily reduce the carbon footprint of bringing everyone to New York. We don't have to jet presidents to far-off countries; we do it for a reason. Think about how many historic photos there are of two former enemies shaking hands to confirm a new deal. How reassuring it is to see their faces together, their hands clasped.

I saw a commercial not long ago about a busy executive dad whose spouse used her smartphone so dad could "be there" at his daughter's recital. "Yeah, right," I scoffed. "That'll make the kid feel really good and give her a memory for a lifetime."

If you think back, pretty much everything pre-Alexander Graham Bell was done in person. Life was, by necessity, entirely local and people relied on neighbors they knew and trusted. Food was sown, nurtured and harvested by people interacting with nature in person. Before today's daycare systems, it was up to grandparents, and those who didn't work in the fields, to take care of the little ones. People gathered as friends and neighbors to celebrate the season and share their news. People traded with their neighbors for items they needed.

Showing up wasn't just a cliché; it was essential to existence. Knowledge, history and skills were learned through personal exchanges. Mother Nature taught us well; hers are lessons that we should hang on to.

Have you ever seen a bird or other animal training its young by example? I live on a lake and wild ducks make their home out in front each spring. The female disappears and, some weeks later, returns with up to a dozen ducklings in tow. This year, one mother duck brought a record seventeen ducklings home! No matter how few or how many she brings, they only seem to know as much as their mother has taught them. As the summer goes on, these tiny creatures stay within a few feet of momma duck, mimicking her every action. She is present and she is teaching strictly through example. Without her there, her cute, little babies would be lunch for any number of predators waiting for her to leave them unattended. This yearly ritual is a marvel to watch and, at the same time, a great life lesson about being present.

How often have you heard someone at a funeral lament that they wish they had spent more time with the deceased? Have you said it yourself? I am guilty, too.

My aunt passed at ninety-eight. She lived in a seniors' home just two miles from my place. I'm ashamed to admit that I found it hard to see her even once a month, though each visit was a delight. We did part with a loving relationship and wonderful memories. I could have done more. I guess I was just too "busy," and my busyness caused me to miss some precious time with her that can never be recovered.

How often do you wake up in a fog, leap out of bed, deal with the kids, deal with your partner, deal with the dog, hose yourself down, throw on your clothes, run to the car, maybe with food or maybe not, so you can join the traffic; or run to the public transit somehow grabbing a coffee along the way, thinking about all the people you miss or tasks left undone, make it to work, get to your spot, deal with what's waiting, grab another coffee to fuel you for the treadmill you are on; and then sometime around 11 a.m., as you realize you are starving, take a moment for yourself to smooth your hair, adjust your clothes, take a deep breath and feel that you have finally stopped vibrating?

Yes, that was a massive run-on sentence. But we have massive run-on days when we are just too busy and miss some of life's important moments or opportunities!

If this sounds familiar, believe me when I say, "The most important person to be present with, in terms of your personal and professional success, is You!"

In this chaotic world, non-stop action can often take the place of actually being present. My dad always said, "Phillip, do one thing well instead of three things poorly." I am still trying to heed his advice.

"It's busy up there," my wife will say and point to my head after I switch topics five times in three minutes, sing a random song, or rattle off some story about a character that suddenly occurred to me.

One of the great things about writing is that I can focus when I write. The flow of words from brain to fingers seems to block out everything else — a great relief and a great discovery for me. I am truly in the moment when I write. I can completely lose track of time. That is a wonderful feeling and I hope you have something you do that allows you to be truly present.

Once you know the feeling of 100 percent presence in anything, you can start to try to translate that feeling to other parts of your life and increase your presence there. Everything you need to succeed is already within you, or very near your fingertips. Just slow down a bit and look around.

Do me, no, do yourself a favor. Tomorrow, and every day when you wake up in the morning and place your two feet on the floor, say "Thank you." Be thankful for the gift of being alive!

Take a breath.

Do a big cat-stretch.

Feel the morning.

Visualize your success that day.

If you have a partner, think loving thoughts or, better yet, say a few loving words to them.

All this in under 60 seconds.

There is nothing, other than a real emergency, that can't wait for 60 seconds.

Now say aloud or think to yourself, "Am I present? Have I shown up yet?"

I believe that just this simple exercise, and these few words and questions, can truly change your life in every aspect.

It's time to really show up and bring your gift of presence.

TWENTY-SIX

KINDNESS — has to be the last word.

In the song lyric "You've got to be cruel to be kind," they get it all wrong.

I believe, instead, that you have to be kind to be kind.

If half the world population did something kind for the other half tomorrow, and the day after that the second half reciprocated, we would be off to a very good start!

I knew that the perfect last word for this book would come to me at the right time. What better way for it to come than through my brother, friend, business partner and mentor. He and I were having a conversation in my office last week, in the building where our father started our company. The way I see it, by he and I being in the same space, with the same genetics and same philosophies, it was a natural outcome that our brains would collaborate and provide the answer.

How perfect.

Kindness, we agreed, is the quality that will bring humanity forward as we continue to evolve.

Getting from when we humans began on earth to where many of us now exist in a modern world took more grit than kindness.

But now, putting "you before me" will take us further than not doing so. We do have a long way to go in that regard, but every kind act we do is a step in the right direction.

My very simple question for you is, are you a kind person or not?

Do you put others before yourself?

At your funeral, would people dwell on kindness as one of your greatest qualities?

Being kind doesn't mean giving up anything. You can be competitive, goal oriented, firm, driven, focused, right or wrong, controlling or any other number of qualities. But each one of them can be governed by kindness.

There is no gray area; you either are, or you are not, kind.

You can't couch it with, "I'm kind, but…."

The song Cruel To Be Kind by Nick Lowe and Ian Gomm may have been catchy back in the late 1970s, but the lyrics were just for entertainment and not to teach a life lesson that is sustainable.

I love hearing about random acts of kindness. That such simple gestures can go so far is awe-inspiring. I think if you look at the text that supports each of the words we have talked about in this book, you will see that the underlying concept is about kindness. To yourself and to others.

Certainly, in times of personal danger or national threats, we need to rely on our "fight or flight" instincts, but that is rare.

We are born to be kind.

We are wired to be kind.

Most people know instinctively when they are being kind and when they are not.

Doing random acts of kindness can be somewhat self-serving because it makes the doer feel so good. The surprise on people's faces when they are the recipients is a wonderful reward. I feel that the ultimate acts of kindness are done with anonymity. It is a small world, though, and even those can come back to the giver, as one did for me a few days ago.

I recently went to an out-of-the-way, local spa to buy my wife a gift certificate for her birthday. It was a quiet morning and the welcoming manager convinced me to get a quick manicure. "No polish!" I insisted, good-naturedly. She agreed, and proceeded to pore over my hands with kindness and care.

A young girl came in to get a pedicure and explained to the owner, as she chose her color, that it was for her prom the following Monday. She declined a matching manicure, saying she only had enough money with her for the pedicure.

While I was paying my bill, I quietly asked the owner how much the manicure would be for the prom-goer.

"Ten dollars."

"I'll pay for it. Please surprise her."

A few days ago, my wife came home with pretty, new fingers and toes. Coincidentally, she had ended up with the same person I had interacted with. During the course of their conversation, my wife learned about my "random act of kindness." She was showered with compliments about how lucky she was to have such a kind husband!

Need I say more, fellows?

Surprisingly, the place where I see the greatest challenges in the kindness realm is often between life partners. I overhear or witness the nicest couples jabbing each other with little digs and I wish they would hit each other with positive affirmations instead.

Another place that kindness, or the lack thereof, has a major impact is in the workplace, where we spend so many hours with the same people and do build deep relationships. Think about how nice it feels when you get complimented in front of your peers or co-workers. Now think how lousy it feels to take a dig from the same people.

These digs can happen without ill intent. I fell into one the other day with a long-term employee who I have the highest regard for. I would never disrespect him, let alone in front of his peers, but I did. It was a busy day and it just happened.

We chatted about the incident together today and I apologized. "Can you believe it?" I asked. "And I am the guy writing a book about this stuff!"

Being disrespectful or dismissive is so easy to do, and easy to try to justify, but it's wrong. I will just keep working hard to get better, and when I screw up I will fix it.

Now reflect for a moment, please. Superimpose this discussion about being kind onto withholding kindness, or chipping away at your life partner with unkind words, and multiply it by 100 times to understand the positive or negative impact. When deep personal love is involved, these matters of the heart magnify, the way sun does through a curved piece of glass. Boy, can they burn.

I have heard and used so many justifications for why it's okay to say or do mean things. "Hey if he can't take a joke…" "She knows I am only kidding…" "He does that to me all the time…" "I can take as good as I give …." But in reality, how many people can, or want to? There really is no acceptable excuse for avoiding kindness.

Why is it that humans have such a hard time with kindness between each other?

We will stop our car for some ducks. We will send a fire truck to rescue a cat. We will help a stranger who has been in an accident. We will nurse a baby animal by feeding it through the night with a syringe, but be kind to my brother, my neighbor or my life partner? Hold on now, that's pushing it!

Perhaps our grit and awkwardness with kindness is still etched somewhere deep in our DNA that helped us get this far. Recall that pewter beer mugs had glass in the bottom so that one's mate wouldn't kill him while he was in his cups!

It occurs to me as I write this chapter that I have witnessed the greatest of kind acts from strangers or friends at a birth or a death. The calls, cards and visits I experienced at both those times often brought tears to my eyes. It's a great lesson that can be built upon once it has been experienced.

My father died in 1996. Dad had driven Cadillacs for many years and most had been white. When we exited the funeral home for the procession to the cemetery, I was moved deeply when my best friend of decades pulled in behind the black cars in a white Cadillac. He had rented it and driven in from out of town as a show of respect and admiration.

With the birth of my first child, I was blown away by the distant friends or peers who took time to handcraft beautiful gifts. A high-school friend — from I won't say how long ago — knit a beautiful, custom, baby sweater. A fairly new employee crocheted the cutest, most detailed, tiny sweater and hat. Dozens and dozens of others showered our growing family with thoughtfulness and warmth that were all based on them being kind for the simple joy of being so.

The web site www.randomactsofkindness.org says they are inspiring people to practice kindness and pass it on to others. They promote a World Kindness Day, saying no matter where you are, this is the day to change the world with one simple act of kindness.

Maybe kindness is my final word because it means so much to me. My late mother was truly kind and gentle with me. She was my world, lost too soon. With her went all that kindness that fills a young man's heart and soul as only a mother's can.

I became a little boy who could often be mean to protect myself, I guess. Thankfully, and with so much appreciation to those who have helped me along the way, I tuned into kindness and work hard displaying it every day.

As the great American poet, Robert Frost, wrote, "…and that has made all the difference."

If the road you travel is bumpy and etched with lack of kindness, I ask you to look far down the other road. The one less traveled that perhaps beckoned but that you didn't take. It is never too late to change direction.

Be amazed and savor the sweet response you will get from being kind.

As with all of the suggestions in *26 Words*, I encourage you to start with small steps and see what happens. You can always travel back to your old trail if you don't like the results. You can even experiment on strangers who will never know you are gauging their reactions to your acts of kindness.

I hope that one of the adjectives that does describe you at your funeral is that you were a kind person, no matter what else you do or accomplish in your life.

AFTERWORD

I have been blessed to have people and knowledge come into my life at just the right time to help me and maybe, just maybe, I will play a small role in your life's journey.

One of the most gratifying things about writing or public speaking is the feedback I receive from my audience. I want to share one final story that will stay with me for life and keep me reaching out to share my learning with others.

The evolution of *26 Words* came out of my desire to pursue more public speaking opportunities. I had been booked for three keynote talks where I would be the first speaker in the morning at a series of conferences.

Having been to many such conferences myself, I knew that I had to come up with something that would compete with the audience's grogginess, the coffee, the pastries, the fruit, the tea and the influx of emails many deal with first thing in the morning. It's not easy to focus on a speaker for 90 minutes when you're barely awake.

I pulled material from a previous talk called "A Few Things That I Have Learned in Life and Business" and put 13 slips of paper in a black magician's hat. Each slip had one word on it, many of which made it into this book. I love audience participation, so rather than me deciding on our journey that morning, I told the audience that they would select the topics. That got their attention.

We did a few audience-wide warm-ups that forced people to be alert or be caught off guard.

Then I walked into the crowd with my hat and let someone pick a word. I was completely without a script and had to take whatever word the person picked and "free-form" with it.

Talk about walking a tightrope without a net at 8 a.m.!

I had also added a few fun words or sayings that got a few laughs, including "$20 bucks." When it was drawn, I gave the person a $20.00 bill. That seemed to wake people up even more.

Well, I have to say that, despite the pressure on me to take words at random and create something special and compelling for the audience, it went pretty darn well. I found out later that I was selected as that sponsor's most popular speaker of the year.

The real highlight, though, was when a lovely young lady came up to the table where I was signing copies of my novel, *Critical Care*, afterwards. She thanked me for the talk and told me her name for the signing. As I was inscribing her copy, she leaned down and said, "You may just have saved my life today."

She looked at me through moist eyes and smiled sheepishly. I was stunned. As I handed her the book I simply said, "Thank you. Whatever it is that you are dealing with, I wish you well in your journey." She walked away, although that moment will be with me forever.

As I drove home and reflected on the talk that morning, I really felt that I had hit upon something; one word really could change a life of another as it had for me. Thoughts of wanting to let that concept be taken further was the genesis of this book and how it came to be.

Now you know the story of *26 Words*.

I am well aware that there is a plethora of other words that can instantly or slowly change our lives. Many other title words competed for space on these pages. I suspect, as you read this, you thought of or wrote down your own. There are words from all aspects of our human existence that, each by themselves, could have a gargantuan impact on any of us.

The 26 words I eventually chose were meant to be relatable in nature. As I wrote, I kept myself open to what my inner bird urged me to share — personal thoughts, awakenings, anecdotes and musings that might resonate with you.

The main point that I hoped to make was that one word, one sentence, one instant of your time can change your life, or someone else's, forever.

If I have touched you in any way, made you think even a little bit differently, or even just amused you at times, then I have accomplished what I hoped to. I wish you so well in your journey and I thank you for allowing me the privilege of sharing *26 Words That Can Change Your Life*.

SHARE THESE 26 WORDS WITH A FRIEND YOU MAY JUST CHANGE THEIR LIFE!

Email info@26words.com
FAX 613-546-9191 or snail mail

Grace Media Inc.
844 Division Street, Kingston
ON, Canada, K7K 4C3

613-536-9800

Your Name: ______________________________

Address: ______________________________

City: ______________________________

State/Province: ______________________________

Zip/Postal Code: ______________ Phone: ______________

Email (will not be shared): ______________________________

Ship To (if different from above):

____

____

____

Recipient's Name: ______________________________

Address: ______________________________

City: ______________________________

State/Province: ______________________________

Zip/Postal Code: ______________ Phone: ______________

Email (will not be shared): ______________________________

Quantity Ordered? __________ x $20.00 = __________

Plus applicable taxes and $5.00 per book for shipping and handling

Call us for payment or enter information below:

Card Type: ______________________________

Card Number: ______________________________

Expiry: ______________________________

Name on the card: ______________________________